Tracking Information
on Today's Internet

Tracking Information on Today's Internet

A Handbook for Creating
Your Individual Semantic Web

Dirk Stähler

Published by: Dirk Stähler, Gummersbach, Germany www.magaseen.de
Creative Consulting and Editing by: Fred Waskiewicz, Boston MA, USA
Icons provided with the kind permission of Alexander Kahlkopf
www.iconmonstr.com

ISBN-10: 150243783X
ISBN-13: 978-1502437839

I would like to thank my long-standing friend Fred Waskiewicz for his continued support. The English version of this book would never have been possible without his help and constructive feedback during the editing process. Many rough edges were smoothed by Fred's careful attention. I look forward to many more years of inspiring thought exchanges, wherever we meet on the planet.

Furthermore I owe a special thanks to my partner Jeanette for her continual understanding while I spent many weekends on this personal project.

Collection – Analysis – Monitoring

Learn how to utilize the content on the Internet
and make it work for you.

Discover the risks to your privacy
that may arise from these new possibilities.

About the Author

Dirk Stähler is an expert on the comprehensive design of organizations, processes and IT systems. He has more than 15 years of experience in the design of innovative organizational, process and IT-solutions. A particular focus of his work is the opportunities and risks arising from the use of publicly available content on the Internet. Making the Internet a "knowledge engine" and the value of the content inside available for everyone is his personal goal. He supports private corporations and governmental agencies in Europe, the Middle East and North America in gaining more value, based on the creative use of their information technology. He has worked as an assistant professor at various universities, and is a frequent author of articles and books. Within his writings, he covers the methodological and technological challenges everybody faces with modern information technology.

More information at **www.magaseen.de**

About the Editor

Fred Waskiewicz is a retired IT professional, having most recently served as Director of Standards at the Object Management Group (OMG). Fred received a master's degree in Computer Science from Virginia Tech.

Preface

For an hour on September 12, 2013, the United Airlines online booking system allowed passengers to book a lot of flights for zero dollars each. Only taxes and fees were charged. This was caused by an error that occurred while entering new prices into the reservation system. The news of the "special offer" spread quickly on Twitter and Facebook. Fifteen minutes were enough to cause a dramatic increase in United's website traffic. The high amount of online bookings triggered an alarm among the staff on duty in the data center. Immediately, the entire website was shut down for several hours. When the site was up again on the afternoon of the 12th, the "deals" were gone, and visitors could no longer take advantage of these extremely "low prices". Have you booked one of these cheap tickets? No? Would you have done so if you had known about it? Wouldn't it have been nice if someone would have automatically informed you in time about this opportunity? Your next vacation would have been significantly cheaper. United never published exact figures on how many tickets were sold at these bargain prices. One day later, the airline released a statement that although they were not legally bound to, they would accept all bookings made. Similar situations like this one occur on the Internet again and again. However, just a few users are able to benefit from them. The reason is that it is difficult to be at the right "online place" at the right time. For a human being, it is hard to constantly monitor the Internet and have the required information at hand that will provide a unique advantage. We can't monitor the Web constantly. Or can we? At least partly? This is no longer a question. Combining services on the Web that have long been known with some recently developed tools allows you to turn the Web into an even more powerful assistant. Automatically monitoring social networks when rumors about errors in reservation systems occur is just one of the possibilities. And the best thing is, you don't have to be a programmer to use these services. That's what this book is about. It explains current developments regarding the exploitation of content on the Internet. And it helps one make optimal use of it.

Chapter 1 describes the development of the Web from a tool for the military, research institutes, universities and a few IT enthusiasts into a mass medium that "stores" the world's knowledge.

Containing amounts of information and knowledge far beyond what we can easily imagine, and far beyond what can be expressed by counting the number of web pages on the Internet. Get to know more about the different ways of measuring the "size" of the Web.

In Chapter 2, I'll explain why a trip to Hawaii can be arranged at bargain prices using the Internet, even if I cannot organize flights for free. Today, everyone is aware that the Internet plays a major role as a source of information and research in our daily life. This covers a broad spectrum, starting with daily news about events, dealing with the purchase of products and services, and does not end with the monitoring and – sometimes – eavesdropping on our communication. When I started work on this book, it was not yet known that the SCHUFA – a major German credit rating agency – was planning to build profiles based on public Facebook entries that would be used to evaluate the creditworthiness of German Internet users. This practice, common in the U.S., kicked off enormous public protests in Germany, a society generally very concerned about the protection of data privacy. The public outcry was the reason that the project was silently stopped a few weeks later. Also, didn't Edward Snowden's revelations start the discussions on the global analysis of Internet traffic by intelligence agencies? Both cases make it unmistakably clear that today, more or less freely accessible information on the Web plays an important role, whether we are looking for affordable products and services, or monitoring and spying on people. Without access to the extensive content on the Internet, both cases of use would be difficult. That said, the Internet - or better - its content, have come to have an immense impact on our daily lives. Isn't it desirable that everyone uses these valuable resources for himself?

Today, the modern World Wide Web (WWW) offers this opportunity to everyone. The only prerequisite is that the appropriate sources and tools for the exploitation of the Web are known. The World Wide Web, only 25 years old, has gone through various phases. Starting from its first phase when the Web was nothing more than a collection of content similar to a library where only specific books could be looked up, it has progressed over a period of active user participation in the creation and modification of content toward today's emerging "smart and intelligent" network. Many specialists work on this new generation of the Internet, a network in which content will be understood by machines that evaluate the meaning of content based on our individual questions and actively support us in daily life. The particular challenge was - and still is – to teach machines to understand content on the net.

They must be able to distinguish content on the Internet that users are interested in from the tons of junk, which they are not.

For computers, this is an extremely difficult task. But there is progress – dramatic progress! In the summer of 2013, we all learned that the NSA was working on an automated evaluation of the world's Internet traffic. The goal was to understand all of the content exchanges: emails, posts on social networks, phone calls routed via voice over IP on the network, and much more. But the ability to automatically browse the network based on terms and to draw certain conclusions depending on results is not limited to intelligence agencies. Every user is increasingly able to automatically evaluate content on the Internet, and to have it work for him or her. And more and more people are making use of this. There is a tangible financial reason: studies show that users who make clever use of the content available on the Web gain a financial advantage. Studies, such as "Consumers driving the digital uptake" of the IAB Europe Institute, have proven that the most experienced users achieve a financial benefit of up to $2,000 per year compared to users who do not understand the underlying value. This advantage arises from the informational advantage based on the optimal use of the contents on the Internet. Wherever possible, experienced users have the Web automatically support their daily decision-making, something that was not achievable by the average user for a long time. The reason: it was just too complicated. Chapter 3 explains why previous approaches did not work, and the new paths that enable every one of us to harvest the value of the Internet's content. Paths everyone - really everyone - can follow.

For novice users, this is good news. The first few kilometers of the new paths to access the content on the Web have already been developed. We just have to get dressed and lace up our hiking boots. This book shows you how this method was developed over the past several years, and where it will lead us in the near future. It serves as guide for those who want to increase the value they gain from the Internet. And it provides a recommendation for action, such as how to collect content on the Web, select its valuable parts, combine it, distribute it automatically, and much more.

Chapters 4 through 7 introduce the important tools that you need to know. But the book goes beyond detailed manuals for individual tools, for which there are already enough tutorials on the Internet. The aim is rather to show how the clever combination of freely available tools and content on the Internet can dramatically increase the profitability of your personal Internet usage. Let the Internet be the watchdog to find the best bargains, researching the latest news about a company, executing recurring tasks and informing you automatically when needed. The tools are available. And even better: most of them are free.

But it is also important to note that there is an inherent threat that the misuse of the new tools can impact every one of us. Only when we know the vulnerabilities we can protect ourselves from possible negative effects caused by the new forms of Internet usage. Chapters 8 and 9 explain the battles for the mastery of content between the old and new world on the Internet, and point out vulnerabilities that can lead to an abuse of the new freedom.

We are currently facing a change in the use of the content on the Web. A change only a few have fully recognized. Currently, public debate strongly revolves around the digitization of all areas of daily life, and the increased mobile use of the Internet. Too little is spoken about the central foundation that is a prerequisite and the basis for these developments: the growing content of the World Wide Web and its future automated use by any user. Yet the means for Internet monitoring is not just available to spy agencies - in today's Internet, it is available to everyone, both for legal and illegal purposes. Those who are capable of making the best and fastest (legal!) use of the content on the World Wide Web will draw the most profit from the next phase of its development. This book serves as an introduction, showing you how to utilize some of the tools available free of charge to become an Internet supersleuth.

Dirk Stähler

Gummersbach, September 2014

More than Expected

The Value within the Internet

The origins of the Internet can be traced back to the 1960s. Its development began as part of a research program of the Advanced Research Projects Agency (ARPA), a division of the U.S. Department of Defense under the name ARPANET. It is rumored that the ARPANET was specifically designed for communication between U.S. military forces following a nuclear strike. However, that was not its primary goal. Rather, the idea was to make better use of the limited computing capacity at the time through a nationwide network of military, university and major research laboratories. To connect the existing mainframe computers with each other, the U.S. had to build a comprehensive computer network. A central piece of this connected network was the development of a unified communication technology initiated in the following decade called the TCP/IP protocol. The new protocol revolutionized the communication between computers. With the TCP/IP protocol, it was possible to reliably connect remote computer networks around the world for the first time. It made geographically distributed yet integrated network structures possible. It was during this time that the name "Internet" was born, a name comprised of the first syllables of the words "Interconnected Networks". Until the late 1980s, the network was only used by the military, research institutes, universities, and a few IT enthusiasts. However, despite the limited user base, a problem was already obvious: the more computers that were connected to each other, the harder it was to find anything within the growing network. In 1990, this situation inspired students Alan Emtage, Bill Heelan and Peter Deutsch to develop one of the first Internet catalogs and "search engines" at McGill University. The search engine they came up with was named Archie. In response to a search request, Archie delivered a list of servers on the network where matching content might be found. Direct access to the content wasn't possible from Archie's "search results". It was still necessary to manually search the computers found by Archie, whether the targeted content was really present or not. This complicated process changed with Veronica, a search engine developed in 1991 by students at the University of

Nevada. Veronica enabled the searching and opening of files on remote computers. The only requirement was to use a program capable of reading the data format in which the search results were delivered (Battelle, 2005). Unfortunately, this was usually not the case. Connecting a large number of small computer networks together using TCP / IP technology led to a heterogeneous network with different technologies and incompatible software. In many cases, the data formats used in different parts of the network were incompatible. Although connected, the computers often weren't able to process the data supplied. Burdensome data conversion processes resulted. This can be compared with two people making a telephone call where both are using a different language. The line is open, they can hear each other, but still do not understand what the other person is saying. Direct access to the distributed content on the Internet was often not possible. The question of how digital content, present on different computer systems in different formats, could be made easily accessible for every user had not yet been answered.

In 1980, a consultant at the European Nuclear Research Center (CERN) by the name of Timothy Berners-Lee worked on this problem. At CERN, different computer systems, different data formats, and a permanent fluctuation of scientists and researchers aggravated the exchange and analysis between project teams (Wright, 1997). To make the life of the scientists (at least those within the CERN network) a little bit easier, Timothy Berners-Lee developed a tool called Enquire. It was a kind of digital card box where documents and links were cataloged. It was possible to define key words or phrases within each document leading to related documents, a concept that is well-known today as a hyperlink.

The idea of combining content from different sources referencing each other was not new. In 1945, Vannevar Bush developed a proposal for a machine called Memex, a machine that would present microfilm content to its users in a linked form. Although Memex was never realized, the draft prepared by Vannevar Bush is considered the first description of a hypertext system. In the 1960s, Ted Nelson picked up the ideas and tried to set up a worldwide library of documents linked by hyperlinks. His project was named Xanadu. Although Xanadu was never fully implemented, it provided valuable conceptual ideas for the development of hypertext systems (Wolf, 1995). In developing Enquire, Berners-Lee was inspired by the ideas of Bush and Nelson. Although he developed a working hyperlink system at CERN, Enquire never reached a point of sustainable dissemination and exploitation. The reason for this was that Enquire was cumbersome and required extensive maintenance. For example, if a document was deleted, all references to the document within other sources had to be removed as well. Invalid references were not allowed. All links leading to documents had to be up to date at all times. Even within the CERN network, this condition was extremely difficult to ensure. The consistency of the overall system simply couldn't be guaranteed. But Berners-Lee did not limit his plans to CERN. During the development of Enquire, he discussed the issues of hypertext systems with experts regularly. He was particularly driven by the question of whether a hypertext system could be extended to the whole Internet. All of the experts with whom he spoke were of the opinion that this was not possible. The reason given was that a global hyperlink system needed to avoid "dead links" on the Internet, or in other words, links to deleted content could not exist (Wright, 1997). To implement this plan, a superior authority - a Clearing House – would be required that ensured the worldwide consistency of the overall system at any given time. The experts considered establishing an agency responsible for the monitoring of links on the entire Internet, which of course was impossible. Their conclusion was that a global hypertext system was impossible, a conclusion Berners-Lee was about to prove false. But in the meantime, the idea of a global hypertext system remained a vision.

Meanwhile, at one point, a scientist at CERN was in search of a floppy disk, which was still expensive those days. In searching for the disk, he evidently found the one on which Enquire was stored. It wasn't possible to determine by whom, when, or for what reason Enquire was deleted. But one day it was simply gone (Palmer & Berners-Lee, 2001).

At the end of the 1980s the Internet made tremendous progress. Although still used mainly by scientists and IT enthusiasts, access to the Internet was now possible for a growing number of users. But the problem of linking content together and accessing it using different computer systems was still an issue. It took ten years before a simple but powerful idea solved the problem of broken links, referencing documents in the "nowhere". It was an idea by Timothy Berners-Lee, who had returned to CERN, that provided the solution. He eliminated the problem of links pointing to documents on the Web that no longer existed, which he called "dangling links", with a simple trick. *"I realized that this dangling link thing may be a problem, but you have to accept it"*, Berners-Lee told a reporter from the Time Magazine in 1997 (Wright, 1997). Only when it is no longer necessary to ensure that all relationships of content on the network are consistent at any time, and when you are willing to give up the idea that search results will always lead you to existing data, only then is it possible to create a world-wide data network without the need of a central controlling authority functioning with a large amount of subscribers. Besides the possibility of linking data within such a network, there is still the requirement of a unified method to exchange content between different computer systems. To address these issues, Berners-Lee developed the key components of today's Internet: a language for describing (HTML), a standard for exchanging (HTTP) and an address system for the unique identification of content on the web (URL System). With these components, he invented the World Wide Web. Without knowing it, Berners-Lee laid the foundation for a worldwide revolution for the creation, distribution and use of information. With his invention, he simplified access to the world's knowledge for a large number of people. It is exactly this knowledge, derived from the individual use of the content on the Internet, that contains incredible value for everybody. Not only ideally, but also financially. Everyone can make use of the value on the Internet. And the best thing is, they can do it almost for free. It is only necessary to access the Web and use the content that has specific value for you. But only if access and use is legal, of course. The value is reflected in the success and development of the WWW into a mass medium for almost every individual. In order to develop a sense of this importance, it is not enough to ask the simple question: How big is the Internet? This question leads directly to further questions. What exactly is meant by the size of the Internet? The number of users? The number of Internet-connected devices? The number of available websites? The amount of generated and stored data? The amount of data exchanged over the Internet? Although answers to these questions cannot completely demonstrate the importance of the Internet within our modern world, they will at least express the visible results of this importance. Let's answer them one after the other.

The Internet by Numbers

Number of Users on the Internet

In 2012, 2.3 billion people had access to the Internet (Internet World Stats, 2012), meaning more than 30 percent of the world's population uses the Web. This number will increase dramatically in the coming years. The main reason for this is the rapid proliferation of wireless Internet. A 3G network cell can already serve up to 200 active users simultaneously. Setting up comparable coverage using a cable network would require up to 200 connections. The cost to build the infrastructure for the mobile use of the network is significantly lower than the cost of burying cable networks underground. This can be compared with the advantages of an air traffic infrastructure over the railroad network. Two miles of railroad tracks are only good for two miles of travel. Two miles of a runway can take us anywhere. And the possibilities for further growth are far from being fully utilized. In 2011, 4.3 billion people owned a mobile phone. Only 824 million of them use the mobile Internet (Accenture, 2011). The rest are future customers. The increased usage of next generation network technologies like LTE will do the rest.

Number of Connected Devices

Using a not entirely legal approach, an unknown hacker surveyed the Internet in September and October of 2012. He placed software in the network on unsecured computers to determine the number of actively used addresses. According to his measurement, 1.3 billion Internet addresses had been active in the second half of 2012 (Carna, 2013). Behind each address was at least one device with access to the Internet. In reality, this structure often hides more computers that share a public address. Take your own Internet connection as example. Your network connection is visible from the outside as one address on the network, but behind this single address might be a desktop PC, a tablet computer, a smartphone and a laptop connected to the network. In this example, these four Internet-enabled devices use the same network address. Assuming that on average, there are two hidden Internet-enabled devices behind each address, Carna's numbers add up to a total of 2.6 billion devices, a number that is close to the estimated 2.3 billion Internet users published by Internet World Stats (Internet World Stats, 2012).

Number of Websites

Even though it is far more difficult to estimate the number of available sites on the Internet, in order to approximate them, the Dutch IT engineer Maurice de Kunder conducts regular evaluations based on the index of search engines. The size of a search engine index such as Google or Bing allows the number of captured websites to be estimated. According to his estimates, the number of websites indexed by search engines is between 13 and 45 billion. For his calculations, he uses data from the search engines Google and Bing. To collect the data, he sends standardized and consistently formulated questions to the two major providers every day, and evaluates the reported results. The calculation of the index size is carried out as a combination of the statistical frequency of words in the query text, the number of reported hits, and possible overlaps in the search results (Kunder, 2013). However, it is difficult to derive an exact number of available sites on the

Internet from these results. First, the calculations vary greatly depending on the order in which the results of a search engine are analyzed. And second, not to be underestimated, all of the websites not recognized by search engines remain uncounted.

Amount of the Generated and Stored Data

Even more difficult is the estimation of annually generated and stored digital content. Since 2007, the market research firm IDC has created an annual estimate as part of its "State of the Universe" study. To calculate the numbers, the IDC analysts use a method developed at the University of California. In a first step, the number of devices capable of generating or storing digital content is estimated. This step covers individual computers, digital cameras, servers, sensors, surveillance cameras, RFID chips, bar-code readers for packaging, and much more. For each class of device, the average amount of digital information it could possibly generate during the period of one year is estimated. This average yields a digital density per device class. For example, the figure for digital cameras is calculated as the product of their average resolution, the average number of generated images per camera per year, and the number of digital cameras used worldwide. Finally, the extent to which this digital data is redundantly stored or copied is estimated (Gantz et al., 2007). For 2011, the analysts came up with an estimated amount of data of 1.8 zettabytes (Gantz & Reinsel, 2011). In terms of MP3 files, this would be enough memory for 3.8 billion years of music. But not all of this data ends up on the Internet. By far the largest amount of digital data remains stored in closed systems ranging from private memory cards carrying the photos of the last vacation, to huge databases of companies and public institutions. However, the IDC experts have shown in successive years that the growth rate of the data generated by digital devices correlates with the growth rate of transported and stored data on the Internet. A tighter integration of networking and external services (e.g. the Internet of Things and Cloud Storage) will contribute to this. However, the methodology used to estimate the volume of digital data produced annually is based on many assumptions, and thus the figures carry a high degree of uncertainty. Nevertheless, estimation methods, as in the example above, are the only way to get an idea of the volume of data generated annually on the Internet, and at least come close to describing that data.

The Visible and Invisible Web

Every estimate of the size of the Internet becomes even more speculative when, besides the visible Internet, the invisible parts of the Web are taken into consideration as well. Simply stated, the visible parts of the Internet can be accessed without any special knowledge. Computers in the visible part of the Internet have a public address and respond when they are called. The public address of a computer in the visible part of the network has a lot in common with a public telephone number you can get from telephone directory assistance. Everybody who can provide sufficient and accurate information about a searched participant on the telephone network receives the phone number from directory assistance unless it is an unlisted number. It is the same with computers in the visible network. Whenever you provide sufficient and accurate search criteria, a search engine will provide you with information about associated computers that store this content somewhere on the Internet. This does not necessarily mean that the attempt to retrieve content from one of these computers will be successful. Just as not everyone arbitrarily called by phone is willing to talk to you, not every computer that is visible on the network is willing to answer your request. Those of you who have ever encountered the "Access Denied" message within a browser know what I am talking about. The "Census and survey of the visible Internet" from the University of Southern California determined in 2008 that there were around 60 million stable, accessible servers on the Internet (Heidemann et al., 2008). Search engines find these computers. Their content is reflected in the index of a search engine, and the results will be included in the search results of Google and others if the targeted computers allow themselves to be indexed.

But in addition to the visible servers that are indexed by search engines, there is another invisible network. The name of this invisible part of the Internet is Dark-Net, or Deep-Net. Compared with the telephone network, we are talking about connections with a "secret number". Content stored on these servers will not be recognized by search engines, and never appear in search results. There are many reasons for this. It may be that a server is not associated with any other website on the Internet, and therefore is not referenced. This is unusual, but can happen. Because most search engines today build an index catalog of the Internet based on links between websites, websites not referenced will not be found. Also, servers that can be identified on the network but prevent access to their content by protection mechanisms belong to the invisible network by definition. Among other methods, this can be achieved by placing information on a web server especially for search engine bots, and then commanding the bots not to capture the stored content. Another part of the content on the invisible network is caused by dynamically created web pages. These websites are created individually for a user at exactly the moment in which he or she sends a request to a server from a browser. For example, a product search on a price comparison website delivers the results individually for a specific user query. The resulting pages are temporary, and exist only for a short time. Therefore it is difficult – and in many cases absolutely worthless – for search engines to index this information. Eric Schmidt, Executive Chairman of Google, estimated the size ratio between the visible and invisible web at the National Advertisers Association Conference in 2005. According to Schmidt, the data collected by Google up to that date supported the assumption that the Internet had a size of approximately 5 million terabytes. In 2005, Google had indexed only 170 terabytes (Plesu, 2005). If Eric Schmidt's estimates were correct, even Google would have indexed less than 0.004 percent of the entire Internet in its database at that time. Unfortunately, we do not have a better figure than Schmidt's estimate.

Amount of Data Exchanged on the Internet

Equally difficult is the determination of the amount of digital data transported over the Internet. The network supplier Cisco estimated that in 2012, the average monthly data exchanged totaled 43.5 exabytes (Cisco, 2013), the digital equivalent of more than 9.8 billion DVDs stacked in a tower reaching 7.500 miles high.

More and more people have access to the Internet, and the number of connected devices on the network is continually growing. Countless websites hold all kinds of content accessible on a global scale in fractions of seconds. Just the estimated 13 to 45 billion web pages on the visible part of the Internet offer 2.3 billion people an almost inexhaustible reservoir of content.

Every Area of Life is Affected

In our personal environment, the network influences how we consume, shop, entertain and collect information. Our work environment has changed dramatically as well, based on new capabilities provided by the Internet. The collection, analysis and processing of digital content is becoming an essential part of many jobs. Knowledge has become an important resource for enterprises and employees. Every production process will be transferred into a knowledge process in which digital content helps create new customer value (Cachelin, 2012). Timothy Berners-Lee's vision of simple and rapid access to the knowledge of the world for a large number of people has become a reality. According to the numbers stated previously, the WWW is definitely a success story, a success that is based on the fact that every user can access content on the network at any time and place, and derive knowledge from that information. The Internet offers a competitive edge for anyone who is capable of using its content, compared with the disadvantages of someone who has no access to these resources. Accessing content on the network determines success or failure. This is true for private and professional environments, such as social networks, wikis, blogs, forums, news portals, search engines, comparison portals, business directories, and many more. But it is not the services themselves that contain value. Rather, it is the content that is found and used by leveraging those services. As consumers, we find bargain deals on products and services that we would have had no knowledge about without accessing the global market on the Internet. We replace previously expensive services with cheaper and sometimes free offers, such as Internet-based communication. Advertising finances the delivery of most of these offers to users free of charge. Ad-supported Internet services deliver an average financial value of $650 (all figures in U.S. dollars) per year per household. The entire value for consumers delivered by Internet-based services is estimated at almost $130 billion per year (IAB Europe, 2010).

But the survey revealed another interesting fact. The financial value consumers derive from the content of free digital Internet services is extremely unequally distributed. A total of 20 percent of Internet users reap 60 percent of the total value of web-based services (IAB Europe, 2010). Based on this distribution, every household belonging to the 20 percent of experienced Internet users gains a total of roughly $2,000 per year. This is a "digital value add" that goes unused by many users every year. A good example is the amount of money that can be saved by the use of price comparison sites. Those who have no access to the data of such services, or use them inadequately or poorly, are giving away money every year. For example, users that are inexperienced in dealing with the content provided by price comparison sites pay on average 16 percent more for electronic products compared with experienced users. This is a tangible example reflecting the *"digital divide"* (Baye, Morgan, & Scholten, 2003).

What Do the 20 Percent Do Differently?

In principle, everyone - at least in the Western hemisphere - with an Internet connection is capable of accessing the content available on the Internet without any restrictions. But it's not the basic access to the Internet that matters. This is just a prerequisite. Really valuable content is often not found by many. The reason is that the traditional ways we used to obtain information on the Internet provide increasingly worse results. It is becoming more and more difficult for search engines to filter and present the increasing amount of content appropriately. Instead, they promote confusion. The problem is the huge amount of results delivered. Increasingly, the overwhelming amount of results leads to *"information overload"* (Carlson, 2003). Search engine operators recognize this situation as well. Since February 2012, the growth rate of searches through major providers has declined. In the autumn of 2012, it was negative for the first time. Google, Bing and Yahoo received 4 percent fewer searches in October 2012 (Thomas, 2012). In certain cases, search engines alone seem to no longer offer any help. And consciously or unconsciously, users seem to have responded to this condition. Finding good content is becoming increasingly difficult. Often the diamonds in search results are drowned out by a large number of hits. Of course, everyone can occasionally find a bargain on the net: cheap flights found by chance, low-priced electronics products on a website heard about from a friend, and clothing from last year's collection. Most of these successes, however, are not sustainable. They cannot be reproduced. They are flukes. The limited valuable information out there is often hidden by insignificant content. Chris Anderson once described this state as *"random electronic noise"*. Particular areas where there is a nearly unlimited amount of content available just a few mouse clicks away are becoming an increasingly larger problem (Anderson, 2006). The

20 percent of experienced users make better use of the Internet because they behave differently. They perform considerably better because they use existing services on the network intelligently. They succeed in gaining a high financial benefit from the content on the Internet despite its permanent increase and change (IAB Europe, 2010). A clever combination of the power of the Internet allows them to generate lasting benefits. The modern Web actively supports them. Users who continuously collect, analyze, monitor, and - within permitted boundaries - save the content of the Internet have access to high quality information and make better decisions.

The modern Internet supports the experienced user with many services. It keeps an eye on ones personal "digital shadow", compares stock quotes with reactions on social networks, monitors informal communication channels, creates profiles of people, and much more. The possibilities range from desirable and helpful to dubious and illegal. Although it may not seem so at first glance, many of these capabilities are freely available to anyone. In some cases, the required tools have existed for years. With the help of these tools, the Internet can provide us with valuable information almost automatically. Today, you have the chance to let the Internet work for you and obtain additional value from it. With a simple comparison, we have tested whether it is possible to realize the "digital value add" calculated by the IAB based on the intelligent use of the Internet. Read on to find out how the Internet can help you save on a trip to Hawaii.

Saving on Overseas Travel (and much more) with the Help of the Internet

Twenty-five years ago, anybody who wanted to arrange an overseas trip without the assistance of a travel agency faced a significant challenge: a lack of information! From the perspective of a German citizen, it was relatively easy to book a ski vacation in Northern Italy or a cottage in the Netherlands, but booking an overseas trip on your own was a virtually impossible task. For example, if you wanted to book a vacation that included Las Vegas, the Valley of Fire, Bryce and Antelope Canyons, topped with a few days in Hawaii - all without the assistance of a travel agent - you quickly became exasperated. Searching for hotels was a difficult task. Where could you find information about hotels available along the route? Printed travel guides and catalogs from the major tour operators were the only available resources. Requesting information about room availability required phone or fax communication, and it took quite a while until you received a written response, even if the request was answered by fax. In general, requests arrived after a delay of several days or even weeks. And after the room reservations along the planned route were successfully completed, the next hurdle popped up: how to get there. Flights could not be searched or booked without the help of a travel agent. At that point, most European travelers realized that arranging an overseas trip to the U.S. mainland and Hawaii could only be realized using the professional help of a travel agent. In the end, many travelers ended up buying a packaged tour of bundled flights and hotels.

Today, the situation has changed completely. Anyone can arrange this kind of trip down to the level of the smallest detail without external help. We can find, compare and book flights, hotels, car rentals, local tours and much more with a few mouse clicks, turning our trip into a unique vacation. The U.S. website offering airline tickets at discount prices, the local tour guide in the desert of Utah, or the small guest house in Arizona can all be contacted with less effort than visiting your local travel agent downtown. Twenty-five years ago, contacting these providers on the other end of the world was solely the privilege of travel agents. Only they could access the global reservation systems of travel companies and tour operators. They were in control of the content and the information. Today, the information required for arranging an overseas trip is available to anyone with an Internet connection at the push of a button from all over the world. And this works both ways. These days, it is as easy for U.S. citizens to access travel information about a trip to Europe as it is for a European citizen to organize a trip to the U.S. However, this capability has its price. The issue Chris Anderson called *"random electronic noise"* makes it difficult to search the Internet for the best information (Anderson, 2006). With a few clicks, the Internet offers so much content that the overview is quickly lost. The question is how to separate and make the most out of valuable information from the flood of content that threatens to drown us.

The financial benefit that can be realized by an intelligent use of the content on the Internet becomes evident by simply looking at the trip described above. Let's compare the prices for different flight and hotel booking options – usually the most expensive parts of traveling – based on a 21-day round trip tour for 2 people starting in Germany. All prices are based on March 2012 euros converted into U.S. dollars.

The travel options compared were:

1. an individually arranged trip, using only offers found on the Internet without external help;

2. a trip offered by a local travel agent based on individual elements of the itinerary; and

3. a bundled package tour of flights and hotels.

On the Internet, flights from Germany via Las Vegas to Hawaii and on to the Hawaiian Islands were offered for $3,700. A stay of 21 nights in 3-, 4- and 5-star hotels totaled $2,600 when booked individually on the Web. The local travel agency's offer came in at $4,000 for flights, and $2,900 for hotels. A bundled package offering included a 14-day base tour covering Las Vegas and Honolulu, all flights, accommodations and local transfers. To make this offer comparable, an "island hopping week" on Hawaii was added, and the total ended up to be $3,800 per person, which included $2,900 for basic travel, $500 for the extended week, and $400 for the flights on the Hawaiian Islands. In the end, this packaged trip would have cost $7,600 for two people. None of the offers included food and drinks.

The result was so clear that there was really no room for doubt as to which option to choose. The individually-arranged trip based on offers found directly on the Internet was $1,300 cheaper than the bundled package tour. And even worse, the package tour offered – in my opinion – lower flight and hotel quality. Even the local travel agency couldn't match the price. The advantage of the Internet compared with the local travel agent was still $600.

I booked this trip to Nevada, Utah and Hawaii exactly as described in March 2012 for travel in September. I have to admit that in the beginning, the reason to personally arrange the trip was not because of potential savings. This approach was simply the most convenient way to choose flight times and airlines based on my individual preferences, and to pick the hotels I wanted to stay in. Only breaking down travel plans into the smallest meaningful parts gives you the freedom to customize your tour exactly the way you want. And surprisingly, this resulted not only in higher trip quality, it produced convincing quantitative results as well, results that were much better than a package trip – of course not difficult to achieve – and even better than a trip arranged by a travel agency.

At this point, an argument is often raised that studies show that booking with a local travel agency isn't more expensive than booking a vacation on the Internet (Stiftung Warentest, 2010). This is true, but only if you compare local travel agencies and the major online travel sites. In these cases, there is often no difference between the prices of the local agent and the Internet. But if you start to reach out for the unlimited global offerings on the Internet, the picture changes. Somewhere in the vastness of the Internet, there is always the best price for every single part of an individual trip. And the more complex the trip and the smaller the building blocks, the less likely it is that a single online travel site or local travel agency will offer the best price. The reason for this is that neither can leverage the full potential of the content on the Internet. They do have access to a large number of offers, but not nearly to everything that is out there on the Web. And in some cases, they don't even want to show us the best prices because this might end up in lower commissions for them. We have to take action on our own. But how can we make use of the almost unlimited content on the Internet without having to spend our days online searching for the information that fits? Once again, how do you separate the valuable information from the flood of content that threatens to drown us and make the most out of it?

It would be next to impossible to manually search hundreds of websites and find the best offers on the Internet without the aid of automated analysis and comparison. The Web has to help us by automatically executing searches and price monitoring tasks based on a few specifications we choose - requirements we define individually and not based on a functionality that is built into a website that we cannot control.

Profit, which is derived from combining content from different sources on the Internet and automatically collecting information with the best cost-benefit ratio, is not limited to the travel industry. The more complex your desired purchase is and the higher the degree of detailed information required to make the right decision, the less traditional search approaches will be able to help.

Whenever the collection, analysis, monitoring, storage and combining of individual pieces of information on the Internet is required, conventional manual content search approaches fail. We need comprehensive pre-filtering to avoid losing track due to *"random electronic noise"*. This situation might change in the future after there has been more progress made on artificial intelligence, but for the time being, we need digital assistants to take care of the pre-filtering of content based on our individual specifications. An example might be an assistant that informs us about United Airlines offering a "bargain" again, but only if we are specifically interested in this information. Only with an Internet that actively supports us by answering our individual questions will we be able to spot valuable information among the increasing amounts of "second class" content. And there is a second requirement the intelligent Internet must comply with: it must be as easy as possible to set up these automatic agents. Let's have a look at the common approach to creating such an intelligent network and the reason why a lot of the ideas behind it fail. And while we're at it, let's try to define the requirements for an intelligent network that really works.

Leverage the Content on the Internet

A Network that "Thinks"

In 1990, the National Science Foundation released the Internet for commercial use, making it available to a broader audience. This meant that in addition to scientists, the military, and computer scientists, "ordinary people" started to discover the power of the Web. Due to the World Wide Web, HTML, HTTP standards, and the URL system developed by Timothy Berners-Lee, it was possible to access the Internet with a simple web browser without the need for deep technical knowledge. It was no longer necessary to acquire details about the technical foundation of a network to access the content provided. The entering of a simple WWW address was all that was needed to have the requested information brought up on your own computer. However, the roles of content providers and content users were clearly divided. Although the network covered a constantly growing amount of topics, the ratio between content consumers and content providers was unevenly distributed. Many consumers were "fed" with content by only a few providers. In other words, most of the early users accessed the content on the World Wide Web in a "read only" mode. Also, available web pages were uniquely separated, comparable to a large number of printed pages placed next to one another and connected only by links leading from one page to the next, and where appropriate, back to the previous page. In its first period of life, the World Wide Web was flat (Hay, 2010). This phase lasted approximately from 1990 to 2000, and is now known as Web 1.0. Basically, the Web 1.0 was nothing more than a large library. Anyone with access could view, and with a little effort even copy the content, but not much more. Timothy Berners-Lee called it the *"Web of Documents"*. Early search engines such as Altavista allowed one to search the network for specific key words, and improved the orientation of the "normal" user within the constantly growing amount of content. If you used the right keywords, chances were good that a searcher could find some matching and interesting content (Rubin, 2009). But this produced an unintended side effect: it became easy to lose yourself on the Web. I still remember my first experiences with the World Wide Web in 1995, spending hours in front of the browser, jumping from one web page to another and ending up somewhere without remembering what I had actually started looking for. The search engines identified too much "exciting" content. Too many promising links on the results pages offered even more interesting content. It was easy to get completely distracted by disconnected but appealing content, navigating from one web page to the next while still attempting to do a serious search. More than once I noticed in the evening that I had spent the day perusing entertaining, but very unproductive content. The WWW seduced the searcher into passively consuming every piece of content that somehow looked interesting. But despite this unproductive side effect, the importance of this first phase of the World Wide Web must not be underestimated. With the spread of the technological base, comprised of HTML, HTTP and the URL system, this phase laid the foundation that made access to digital content available to almost everybody worldwide, regardless of the computer systems and networks used. The Web 1.0 opened up the availability of the scattered knowledge in the world and facilitated its access.

By the year 2000, two developments triggered a change in the use of the World Wide Web. The first change was driven by new technologies, which made it possible to simply mash up content from different websites onto one single page. Instead of sending visitors away from a particular web page using external links, web page owners increasingly collected this external content and presented the "mashed results" on their own web pages. With this new approach, websites could be designed comprehensively in terms of content without having to worry about generating all of the material presented. The solutions ranged from simple integrations of additional information, such as the local weather forecast, up to the development of comprehensive commercial offers based on data collected by third party systems. In many cases, this approach obviously led to legal disputes. A case that attracted public interest in Europe was the dispute between the European low-fare airline easyJet, and two price comparison websites that had accessed the pages of the airline and used the data within their own offerings without permission.

The second change affected WWW users who until then had passively participated in content consumption. For the first time, it was possible to easily leave comments or edit other web pages (Hay, 2010). Technologies such as wikis, blogs, forums, and social networks made the direct involvement of each user possible. Darcy DiNucci used the term Web 2.0 for this second phase of the World Wide Web development for the first time. In 1999, she pointed out that the Web 1.0 we had seen so far was just a prototype of the interactive network that would permeate many areas of our lives in the future (DiNucci, 1999). Suddenly, content creation was no longer limited to a few experts. Everyone could participate in its creation and editing without in-depth technical knowledge. That's why Timothy Berners-Lee called the Web 2.0 the *"Web of Content"*. It democratized the creation, manipulation and use of content. And it enabled participation.

Beginning in 2010, the Internet entered its next phase of development: Web 3.0. Today, nobody can define exactly what the Web 3.0 is, or what it will look like in the future. But it is certain that significant changes have occurred, requiring a distinction from its previous phase. David Siegel describes it as a network that is increasingly intelligent and becomes a computer itself (Siegel, 2010). Individual hardware and software will become less important. The interaction of distributed components within the Internet will gain considerable significance. How this might look on a larger scale in the near future has already been demonstrated by smartphones with augmented reality solutions. By combining a GPS receiver, a camera, a mobile Internet connection, and globally distributed servers, new information solutions have been made possible. Updated in real time, it is possible to mash up local information collected with a smartphone camera with content provided by servers on the other side of the globe. Whenever you point an augmented reality app on the Berlin Cathedral, for example, it is easy to receive information about the building and its history, informatively embedded in the image of the smartphone's camera. The main computational work for this interaction is executed on computers provided by different providers via the Web. The smartphone's primary use in this scenario is locating a position, sending requests, and displaying results. Without an "intelligent network", solutions like this one are not feasible. Google has taken this approach to the next level with the development of its Google Glass. Even though Glass has caused some discussions about privacy, there will be more and more specialized devices throughout the network that are connected, building a greater whole in the near future.

Of course, the statement that "the network will become intelligent" and that "hardware and software will become less important" has to be seen in relative terms. Even the smart grids of connected devices require hardware and software. But a clever combination of distributed resources will be more capable of responding to the individual information needs of every user. For a user, where required information is processed is irrelevant. The only thing that counts is that the right information is collected and delivered.

Therefore, it is crucial that the "intelligent network" knows how to obtain the information. The more the network learns about us, the "smarter" it gets, and thus the better the results. Conrad Wolfram, creator of the knowledge engine Wolfram Alpha, expects the next generation of the Internet to constantly generate new knowledge for the user (Kobie, 2010). In his forecast, the Internet turns into a personal assistant who knows practically everything about "its user", delivering support for every situation in their daily life. The foundation for this will be based on the content and its relationships stored in a *"giant database"* somewhere on the Internet (Strickland, n.d.). Web 3.0 development is therefore not primarily about technically creating a new network. Rather, it is focused on providing solutions that make the content within the network readable for machines. Without the capability to "understand" the meaning of content stored on the Internet, computers will not be able to individually solve problems for us. The aim is to create a "semantic network", a third generation of the WWW, in which machines can "understand" the underlying meaning of content. But if taken literally, the term "understand" is misleading. It's not about artificial intelligence, where computers really "understand" the content. Instead, the idea is to provide content on the Internet in a form that can be interpreted and processed by computers autonomously and without human interaction. The

World Wide Web Consortium (W3C), the organization for the standardization of the Internet, proposed a solution for how this intelligent Web 3.0 could be realized. The work of the W3C defines, how content in the Web 3.0 is defined, will be standardized and relationships between the content will be interpreted by machines.

Within Web 3.0, digital assistants will independently search and evaluate information, and based on the results, will execute tasks automatically. Every activity of these assistants will be focused on the information needs of each individual user (Rubin, 2009). The Web 3.0 is a "thinking" network. It will individually and automatically help us address questions that arise every day. It adds intelligence to the Internet.

You don't think so? Have you ever used your smartphone to find a restaurant, a doctor, a cinema, or a pharmacy in a foreign city? Just add a little more intelligence and the combination of a smartphone with a wireless network and some powerful servers somewhere on the planet might provide you with this information even before you know you need it.

The Difference between the "Web of Documents" and "Web of Data"

Although the terms sound similar, there is a significant difference between the Web of Documents (Web 1.0) and the Web of Data (Web 3.0). The Web of Documents consisted of a static collection of documents, connected mainly by hyperlinks. Content-wise, computers couldn't do much on Web 1.0 automatically. That's completely different with the Web of Data, where machines are capable of analyzing and interpreting content and reacting independently. Take simple text as an example. Within the Web of Documents, the text published on a website was just a bunch of digital ones and zeros for machines. Within the Web of Data, computers can "read and understand" text. For this to work, the original content on a website must be supplemented by analyzable descriptions of the content, similar to the barcode on a product package where there is always a price tag for you as human, and a second tag encoding the price for the checkout scanner. This second code enables the scanner to identify the associated product and look up the price in a database.

The Intelligent Internet

In order to realize the Web 3.0, the content of a website must be provided in a form that allows computers to search for specific information in it, or to derive the information searched for based on this content. Only when this has been ensured will the network be able to execute, at least to some degree, an automated search and interpretation of the content. This is anything but an easy task. Consider the annual reports of Lufthansa and Air Berlin available on the Internet as an example. Both contain detailed information about the economic development of both companies for the year in question. This includes sales, profits, number of passengers transported, strategic planning, growth prospects, and much more. For someone with basic business knowledge, it is easy to assimilate and digest this information while reading the text. Computers, however, have enormous difficulties when it comes to automatically analyzing content and interpreting its meaning. An attempt to automatically extract the key figures of Lufthansa and Air Berlin from their reports, evaluate their meanings, and draw conclusions based on this information is an immense challenge for a computer. Try to compare the number of passengers transported by the two airlines in 2012 by using information from their annual reports. The exact numbers can be found in both reports. But extracting the numbers out of the reports automatically is not possible. Only a closer look at the annual reports provides us with the information. Even if the Internet delivered the reports as a PDF document, you, the human, would still need to perform the essential work of extracting the information. The content must be manually interpreted, compiled and compared by you. The Internet has done nothing more than deliver the digital documents. Nothing was automatically evaluated or interpreted by the network, which is a pure Web 1.0 behavior. Even a direct search - on Google, for example – does not solve the problem in a satisfactory way. Although the search term "compare passengers transported 2012 Lufthansa Air Berlin" provides useful results, you're still required to look up the numbers within the text by yourself. Even the clever Google servers weren't able to provide you with the exact information at the top of the results set. Although this wasn't a complex question, again, we end up in the Web 1.0 world. Having access to the vast amount of content, we still have to do the interpretation of the content and the final search for answers on our own.

The example is transferable to almost the entire Internet. The Internet embodies enormous amounts of content and information. Up to 45 billion web pages on the visible part of the network cover almost every possible subject. But when it comes to interpreting these web pages, in most of the cases, we have to do this on our own. There are, of course, sophisticated solutions that provide answers to individual questions derived directly from the network without any human interaction. With its computer Watson, IBM showed the potential of artificial intelligence that is based on the content of the Internet. Equipped with enormous computing power, modern supercomputer systems can automatically analyze the content of the Internet and specifically derive answers to non-standardized questions. But for the time being, this technology only provides reliable answers in limited areas of application, such as medicine and finance. It will take some time for solutions like Watson to be available for every user on the Internet.

With the Web of Data approach, the W3C primarily pursues a means of providing machine-readable content on the Internet. To bring the idea to life, they defined three central components: eXtensible Markup Language (XML), Resource Description Framework (RDF) and ontologies. The following lines contain a few technical explanations. They are important in order to understand why I don't think that the W3C approach is suitable for broad-based applications on the Internet. Don't be afraid, I will limit the technical details to a minimum.

Component 1:

Extensible Markup Language (XML)

Extensible Markup Language is a language for the structured representation of data. With the help of XML, content can be described in a form that simplifies the processing of data within computer systems, not only on the Internet, but also when it comes to computer communication in general. Taking an airline's annual report as an example, if presented in an XML version, the number of passengers transported could be described at a fixed position within the digital document and marked with a unique designation such as "passengers 2012". If content is described in a form like this, it can be easily found and processed automatically. But there is still a problem. To ensure that XML content can be understood on a broader basis by everyone creating an XML document with similar content, those creating the documents must use the same "marks" to identify specific parts of the overall content. Achieving these standardized document descriptions is often a complicated task.

Component 2:

Resource Description Framework (RDF)

The Resource Description Framework is used to describe the relationships between objects in a dataset. Using our airline example again, imagine it as a list of airlines and a list of the volume of passengers transported in 2012. In order to enable computers to identify which passenger volume belongs to which airline, the content must be related. For a human, it is sufficient that the relevant content "name of the airline" and "passengers in 2012" are printed on the same line. Using our cognitive abilities, we associate the numbers with the corresponding airline. For computers, it is not that easy. They need precise information on how the content in a data set is linked. In our case, that means an exact description of where to find the airline name, the passenger volume, and how both are related. For example, in a digital list of airlines and passenger volumes, the relationship "has transported the volume of passengers in 2012" could be expressed using RDF. If you want to build a structure generically describing the relationships between data, RDF could help. Based on this, a set of data relationships could be interpreted by machines.

Component 3:
Web Ontology Language (WOL)

The special feature of the Internet is that its content is stored on distributed computers connected within a large network. Therefore, combining and linking content from various sources is often required. Again, looking at our example, if you would like to detect the number of Lufthansa and Air Berlin passengers in 2012 automatically, two different sources have to be found, linked and compared on the Internet. In the example, both Lufthansa and Air Berlin call the desired information "passengers". But what happens when one airline calls the information "passengers" and the other "guests" in their annual reports? At this point, ontologies come into play. They describe semantically identical content within different data sets, and the overall relationships across the data sets. In order to make computers "understand" that they are looking semantically at the same content type within different data sets, cross-relationships must be created using ontologies. With the Web Ontology Language (WOL), the W3C has defined a specific language for setting up these relationships across different websites.

Will it Become Reality?

W3C would like to extend human readable content on the Internet. In addition to the Web of Documents (Web 1.0) and to the Web of Content (Web 2.0), they would also like to add a machine-readable level. This third level should strengthen the capability of the Web and enable machines to understand the content on the Internet (Berners-Lee, Hendler, & Lassila, 2001). Machines, of course, do not "understand" content. But if they could base their calculations on assignments and logical relations, automated processing would be possible.

Sound difficult? It is difficult! The technical implementation of a system of XML, RDF and ontologies is anything but trivial for a normal website provider or developer. Although the initial work on the standardization of the Web 3.0 was made at the end of the nineties, very few solutions out there today focusing on specific areas of expertise remain. One example is the Biological Ontology Database of the European Bioinformatics Institute (EBI) that supports researchers in the field of microbiology. This database helps molecular biologists describe research results using a structured and defined vocabulary. Links between the individual works of the researchers can be easily created and new insights easily obtained on the basis of the existing links. It is obvious that this technique is extremely helpful in a well-defined area of knowledge in connecting data sets and data sources. Extended over the content of the entire Internet, the implementation of such a solution, covering the whole content on the Web is – for the time being – an impossible task. How can one structure 45 billion web pages in a digital format (XML), describe the semantic meaning associated with each (RDF), and in the end create semantic links between the different pages (WOL)? In practice, this cannot be realized. That's the reason why the comprehensive semantic web remains a vision to this day. The required structures to enhance a larger number of websites on the Internet with RDF and WOL for automated processing do not exist, and will not exist in the near future (Petrie & Agarwal, 2012). The reason is that extending content created for humans with the standardized RDF and WOL information is extremely work-intensive. The creation of the ontology within a specific area of expertise requires a lot of time. And the complexity grows exponentially compared with the growth of the amount of content. Practice shows that even in the same area of expertise, the overarching link of ontologies is often not created. Take the database of the European Bioinformatics Institute as an example. Faced with operating multiple ontologies that are divided into different sub-areas of interest within the field of microbiology, the EBI prefers an individual approach instead of "one size fits all". How can we expect to implement an overall ontology on the Internet, when even scientists within a specific field of expertise choose a specialized and non-integrated approach in building up their solutions? Don't get me wrong, the use of RDF and WOL within limited areas of expertise is quite reasonable, but a widespread use on the Internet in the near future is highly unlikely.

In March 2007, Stephen Downes, a senior at the National Research Council of Canada, started a discussion on his website with the article *"Why the Semantic Web Will Fail"*, a discussion that continues to this day. According to him, the realization of a comprehensive semantic network would only be possible if producers and content providers would start to work together and - at least partially – give up their individual advantages and profit. Only in this case does he consider the introduction of a standard for the semantic web as possible. But the individual economic interests of the content "owners" will prevent it. Besides the economic argument, he also does not believe that users would like such a system. Content that is standardized and evaluated by machines could facilitate automated profiling. If the entries on Facebook, Twitter, Google and others could be collected, linked and analyzed by every user, he would expect more rejection than acceptance. Downes' conclusion is to retain control over our own content to the greatest extent possible, and not to deliver content into a system whose planned good intentions could not be controlled (Downes, 2007). His article received a great deal of response on the Internet. Comments ranged from approval to disapproval. In an interview I conducted with him in late 2012, he reiterated his position. Additionally, he mentioned that he recently observed yet another change in conjunction with the semantic web: large providers like Twitter, Google and Facebook are moving away from the concept of open data. They are constantly establishing tighter and more controlled access to their offerings. The Internet currently faces exactly the opposite of Timothy Berners-Lee's vision of open content within a Web of Data. Restrictive and closed structures are evolving.

Four Difficulties

In the foreseeable future, a worldwide semantic network is not in sight. More than ten years after Timothy Berners-Lee presented his proposal for the design of such a network, little has changed. The reasons why the W3C idea of realizing a Web of Data across the entire Internet will fail are built upon each other.

Once a single problem is solved, another one appears immediately. Let's consider the main points of conflict one after another.

The Problem of Cooperation

In principle, website owners – especially when operating a site commercially – resist cooperation when it comes to sharing content with third parties. However, making content on the Internet machine-readable, such as through the solutions proposed by the W3C, simplifies accessing third party content significantly. But why should an operator of a website share his content, often created at great expense, without receiving anything in return? Without compensation, usually financially, no operator of a commercial website has an interest in enabling easy access to and use of the site's content. The resistance will be even higher the more valuable the content is! The dispute between easyJet and some online travel services about the unauthorized use of data scraped from the airline's web page shows how quickly situations like these can end up in court. Even if the dispute had been resolved in favor of the online service in this case, it is clear that accessing someone else's content usually triggers reactions on the other side (Ziegler, 2010), reactions that are usually not "take the content and feel free to use it for whatever you like".

The Problem of Costs

If we assume that the problem of cooperation is solved, and every website operator is always willing to provide valuable content without any financial compensation, then the next question arises: who will bear the costs for the extra effort of content preparation (e.g. using XML, RDF and WOL)? The development and maintenance of the semantic web requires additional work for each web page, in addition to the normal part of creating a web page for human consumption. Even if only a minimal expense allowance for the preparation of machine-readable content is charged, most users will not pay for it. Why should they?

The Problem of Coordination

Assume further that both problems – the problem of cooperation and the problem of cost – are solved. Website operators provide their content without any financial compensation and without being paid for the extra effort on their side, making machine-readable content available. Anyone who regards this situation as realistic should think about seeing a doctor. But let's assume for the sake of example that both issues have been solved. The issue now becomes how to build a continuous, well-defined description of machine-readable content spanning multiple areas of expertise within the whole Internet. The design and maintenance of a system that standardizes machine-readable content on the whole Internet requires a clearinghouse that normalizes all structures. Do you recognize anything? This is a similar situation that Timothy Berners-Lee was faced with when he wanted to design a global system for hypertext. In that case, he had to solve the problem with "dangling links" pointing towards pages on the Internet that no longer existed. It was clear at this time that there would be no worldwide clearinghouse that would take care of dead links. And it is very unlikely that there will be such a clearinghouse for ontologies in the near future either.

The Problem of Complexity

Assume that the problem of coordination would be solved as well. In our ideal world, there is some kind of organization that defines and controls the worldwide system of building machine-readable semantics on the Internet - by defining global ontologies, for example. In this case, it would still be necessary to ensure that the complicated process of annotating content for machines, such as with RDF, was carried out correctly by "normal" website operators. Even if we limited our thoughts on the lowest estimate of available websites worldwide, there are still 10 billion pages that must be enhanced accordingly. This figure alone shows that the implementation of this idea is completely unrealistic. No one could ensure that the required labeling has been correctly implemented and maintained.

The Solution only Works in Utopia

The W3C vision for a Web of Data cannot be implemented on a broader basis. To prove this assertion, after the idea was presented by Timothy Berners-Lee in 2001, little has happened. Practice has shown that the approach does not work on a larger scale. Ontologies for a structured description of content on the Internet only exist within a few areas of expertise. Links between different areas of expertise barely exist. Also, RDF is not widely used by website operators. Today, only XML is established as a common data exchange format.

In order to implement the Web of Data, we need a different approach. What might the solution look like? Let us first take a closer look at the problems of complexity and coordination. It cannot be expected that billions of web pages will be overhauled for machine readability according to official standards, whether RDS, WOL or other methods. The problem is similar to the obstacle that stood in the way of the development of the Web 1.0. It is the difficulty that lies within the attempt to create a consistent system valid for the entire Internet worldwide. Only when Timothy

Berners-Lee gave up his approach to solving the problem of *"dangling links"* did the Web 1.0 arise (Wright, 1997). With the Web 3.0, we are facing a similar situation. It is interesting that even Berners-Lee stumbled into the same problem while trying to design the Web 3.0, a problem he successfully solved at the beginning of the nineties by eliminating the key obstacle for the development of a global hypertext system. If we want to realize the idea of a network in which content is understood by machines, we have to supplement the error message "web page not found" with another message: "semantics not found". Only when we accept that – for the time being – there will be no comprehensive and closed system connecting the content on World Wide Web 3.0 to a machine-readable structure can we move on and solve the problem of complexity. Of course, the solutions resulting from this finding will be highly individual. But they will work. They will be better than nothing, and perfectly adequate for the individual user. Any attempt to introduce a single universal method will fail. Or to be more precise, all attempts at such a solution have failed for more than 10 years. We are in need of simple methods and tools to gather content individually on the Internet and provide it in a structured and machine-readable form. Only when every single user is capable of easily creating machine-readable content without deep technical expertise will the Internet come closer to the semantic web.

At that point, a global and valid ontology for the entire Internet will no longer be required (Petrie & Agarwal, 2012). Complexity will be reduced by focusing on the individual content structure requirements defined only by the content users without being required to consider an overall and "worldwide valid" structure. In this case, the problem of coordination will disappear. There will be nothing to coordinate.

Following this approach, the problem of costs will also lose its impact. First, when content is processed individually by the people who want to use it on an automated basis, there will be no additional upfront costs for website operators. Second, it will be much more efficient when users edit content for machine readability by themselves, instead of having website operators do this work upfront (Petrie & Agarwal, 2012). The reason for this is that only the content that has a user benefit will be processed. What is not needed by anyone does not have to be prepared for machine processing. Let's leave it to the principle of a market economy here as well. Only when there is demand will a supply arise. Of course, following this approach, we would "only" end up with individual results, but they would be easily usable for the single user. The problem of costs on the side of content providers and website operators would be solved.

What still remains is the problem of cooperation. If the operators of a website did not want to share content, they would likely make it as complicated as possible to access it in a machine-readable form. Anyone not wanting to cooperate would definitely not grant easy access to the content. But Web 3.0 tools – some have been around for quite a while, some are new –increasingly enable users "to make use" of external content on the Internet. With these tools, the question of content provider cooperation often no longer arises. Content is accessed with or without permission. Of course, legal boundaries must be considered. But website operators would have to accept that it will be increasingly difficult to control or stop the external use of "their" content. The music industry put this to a test and failed. I predict that the next businesses that will fail are magazine and newspaper publishers.

The Individual Web 3.0

In 2001, Timothy Berners-Lee wrote: *"The real power of the Semantic Web will be realized when people create many programs that collect Web content from diverse sources, process the information, and exchange the results with other programs. The effectiveness of such software agents will increase exponentially as more machine-readable Web content and auto-*

mated services including other agents become availa-ble" (Berners-Lee et al., 2001). To realize this vision, the content on the Internet must be prepared individually for automatic processing, linked with other content, used to trigger actions, and – where necessary – stored. At first glance, this appeared unsolvable for the average user, especially if all of the steps have to be combined. Do we have to learn programming now?

A comprehensive and standardized solution implementing the vision of Timothy Berners-Lee will not be seen in the near future. But everyone using the tools available on the Internet can create individually crafted solutions that solve individual tasks without extensive technical knowledge. In most cases, the tools can be used for free. The results will be valuable if we accept what was true for the Web 1.0 and its dead links as well: individually created solutions sometimes stop working from one day to the next, either because the underlying website has been changed structurally, the required tools are no longer available, or the owner of the content implements technical measures making access more difficult. Similar to the Web 1.0, where websites disappeared from one day to the next, resulting in the error message "web page not found", the error message "semantic not found" belongs to the individual Web 3.0. Of course, this is not the semantic web Berners-Lee described as his vision. It offers no standardized basis for the automatic processing of its content. It does not pave the way for a general order of content for the entire Internet. Rather, this individual Web 3.0 enables the next evolutionary step toward the real Web 3.0. Small, achievable steps are much better than an attempt to set up a comprehensive solution that won't progress properly for years. Therefore, it is necessary to approach the problem from a different angle. Let's provide access to the tools that solve the individual user problems of by making use of the content available on the Internet. This approach will advance the Web 3.0 much more than all of the efforts to define semantic standards that have not succeeded for years. With the four central components of collecting, analysis, combination and automation, everything we need is available. Easy access, without detailed technical knowledge, emerged from Web 1.0; the possibility of individual analysis and combination of content emerged from Web 2.0; and an automated network that performs tasks independently is on the rise with the individual Web 3.0. The foundations for this new Internet were already laid a few years ago. Let's find out where it all started.

Content Collection

A Scissors for the Internet

In June 2006, an Israeli software company introduced a tool that enabled access to the Internet's content in a new way. The name of the tool: Dapper. The software engineers Eran Shir and Jon Aizen, the creators of Dapper, described the idea behind the tool on their blog shortly after its release as follows:

"Dapper's mission is to allow you to use any web-based content in any way you can imagine. And by use we mean going beyond just reading or viewing a web page." (Shir, 2006)

With Dapper, a user is capable of extracting content from web pages for further processing. Even more is possible, however. Once a content collection request is defined within Dapper, this collection can be used again and again if the underlying web page hasn't changed. According to its founders, the name of the tool has two different meanings: a "geeky" one, and an inspiring one. The "geeky" one is that Dapper is an abbreviation of "**Da**ta Ma**pper**". The connection to the term "Web of Data" introduced by Timothy Berners-Lee is obvious. The second meaning is inspired by the English word "dapper", a term connoting dignified, neat and elegant. By this, Eran Shir and Jon Aizen wanted to express the idea of Dapper making the network more elegant, well-maintained and accessible for every user (Shir, 2006). Using Dapper, it is possible to convert the content of many websites into a machine-readable form. But the service is not limited to static web pages, meaning web pages where fixed, non-variable content is displayed. It is also possible to extract website content that requires queries to present data individually compiled for the user. Think of a website searching for movies playing at local theaters. Before the web page displays any results, you might have to enter your preferred local theater, the starting time of the movie, and maybe the genre. With Dapper, you can store your individual settings for future content extraction on a regular basis. With this functionality, content that is normally accessible after filling out forms on a web page can be read easily. This functionality allows users to capture dynamically generated content on the Web automatically. And there are more applications for this than local movie show times. Further examples include automatically extracted telephone numbers that belong to a specific name and address, the price of a product or service extracted from a price comparison portal or an online store, new entries of someone you monitor on a social network without being connected with that person, and much more.

Dapper is a valuable tool to find and extract content on the Internet and provide the content in a machine-readable form. The results of a Dapper query can be easily deployed in a form that is suitable for further processing. Imagine this as the production of *"plastic bricks"* out of web page content.

Consider the content of web pages as raw material within the process of building these *"plastic bricks"*. Disassembled into their components, the *"plastic bricks"* can be individually re-assembled afterwards. But before we can start re-assembling parts of the content collected on web pages, we must first create our personal box of *"plastic bricks"*. To build our individual collection, we have to disassemble web pages with a virtual scissors first. That is exactly what Dapper does.

In October 2010, Dapper was sold to Yahoo. After this became publicly known, Eran Shir said that the financial aspect of the decision was subordinate. He explained that the future growth of Dapper, both in commercial and technical fields, could be ensured with this deal, particularly commercial growth based on new revenue in the area of online advertising (Shir, 2010). At that time, Dapper had already gained a loyal community of supporters and fans. Their disappointment with Dapper's focus on online advertising was reflected in many comments on the Internet. Marshall Kirkpatrick perfectly summarized those comments in his blog in October 2010. He complained that whenever there is a gap between a new technology and its not yet completely understood possibilities, advertising apparently becomes the only way to finance new ideas. In his view, the quick attempt to finance an innovative idea with the business model of advertising has destroyed many innovations at an early stage (Kirkpatrick, 2010). But on the other hand, it clearly raised the question: why must innovative companies and the people behind them often have to rely on advertising as a last resort to finance their new ideas?

Lately, the users of Dapper have been increasingly challenged by technical problems. The analysis of web pages often stops, or the service is not accessible at all. The causes of these problems cannot be precisely identified. But it appears that Yahoo seems to have lost its interest in maintaining and enhancing the publicly available version of Dapper. Nevertheless, one fact remains: Erin Shir and his team made an important contribution to the pragmatic implementation of the individual Web 3.0, and inspired many successors. Promoting the ideas of the individual Web 3.0, more and more tools are now available to support the collection and machine-readable preparation of content on the Internet.

A promising alternative had its origins in the Hanoi Social Club in Vietnam, where in August 2013, Pratap Ranade and Ryan Rowe sat in front of their laptops writing the first lines of code for a tool that has the potential to change the way we collect and make use of content on the Internet. Both attended the doctoral program at Columbia University in New York, but dropped out to exchange science for business. Ranade started a career with McKinsey in New York, while Rowe followed an offer from frog design in Shanghai. The company frog design, founded by Hartmut Esslinger in Altensteig, Germany in 1969, provides solutions for product design, digital media and business strategy, and became known through its participation in the design of the first Apple computers back in the early 1980s.

Spending a lot of time on business trips often associated with long distance flights due to their jobs at McKinsey and frog design, in the winter of 2012, Ranade and Rowe had a vision of the answer to a simple question: What movies will be playing on my next flight? While in-flight entertainment listings are publicly available on almost every airline's website, it is always cumbersome to look up the information. There was no single website that summarized the different inflight entertainment programs for different airlines. Since both liked to work on joint software projects whenever their paths crossed, they decided to create a solution to address this problem. After a few months of programming, that solution, named airpapa (www.airpapa.com), went live. Airpapa assists a passenger in finding movies playing on flights by simply choosing the airline, departure and arrival airports and travel dates. At that time, they didn't know that airpapa was the spark that would ignite a much bigger idea.

While developing airpapa, they repeatedly faced the challenge of accessing data sources on the Internet that don't provide machine-readable content. The onboard entertainment program for almost every airline can be found online, but unfortunately, usually not in a standardized format and in a single place. These circumstances forced them to code every required interface individually, a complicated, tedious and extremely time-consuming activity (Forrest, 2014). *"We felt the pain of writing web scrapers first-hand and realized that building and maintaining scrapers was often the only way to get data from the web, but took precious development time away from higher value work"*, explained Ranade. So they created a tool that simplified the scraping of web pages and converted the content into a machine-readable form, although initially only for their own use.

But the two founders recognized another potential application their newly created scraping tool offered. Ranade described the other motivation behind the development of a tool for scraping content from websites that do not provide machine-readable access as follows:

"Observing colleagues at frog design and McKinsey, we realized that we were surrounded by smart people with a good understanding of data and analysis, but no programming ability. Often these would be domain experts, for example, an expert in the Oil & Gas industry with a well informed perspective on what data sets were accurate and what analyses would provide real insight into the industry. We wanted to bridge the gap between talented domain experts like these and programmers by giving them access to the tools that programmers have."

Surprisingly, Ranade and Rowe almost talked themselves out of the idea during the early days.

Fortunately for everyone looking for an easy way to scrape content on the Internet, they became aware that they had something with real potential when the public beta version was launched with a single post to Hacker News in January 2014. The post quickly rose to the top of hacker news, and they received over 5,000 signups in one day.

Looking at the Web 3.0 development, the founders are convinced that it will become a data backbone that powers the Internet of Things, a network of connected devices creating data from multiple sources we interact with seamlessly, often without realizing it, through apps. This will include things like wearable computing devices, smart appliances and so forth.

As explained by Ranade, *"The Web 1.0 was composed of websites designed to be interpreted by people looking at traditional screens. As we move into the world of connected devices, it's more important than ever that all this data is machine-readable and accessible by programs and devices - therefore web data and services need to become APIs (author's note: Application Programming Interfaces enable software programs to interact with each other). Although large 'digital natives' like Facebook and Twitter are proactively exposing APIs, most of the content on the web is not machine-readable accessible. The Semantic Web effort led by Tim Berners-Lee and the W3C tried to address this by coaxing data owners to tag their data with RDF tags. At kimono labs, we are taking a 'crowd-sourced' approach to building a machine-readable Semantic Web. One of the fascinating things about the Internet is how much value lies in its long tail - tons of user generated and niche content that is produced by individuals and small organizations. If the Internet were simply the sum of the largest services like Facebook, Twitter, Google or LinkedIn, it would not be interesting. The long tail provides tons of value and our own user data confirms this (author's note: In statistics, a long tail of some distribution of numbers is the portion of the distribution having a large number of occurrences far from the 'head' or central part of the distribution. Applying this concept to the distribution of valuable content on the Internet, this means that there are millions of niche providers that do not provide machine-readable access to their content). Larger websites and web services will eventually expose APIs, but the long tail will not. We are enabling users to build APIs for the long tail of the web, creating a complete data backbone that will power Web 3.0."*

Choosing a name for the new service wasn't a big deal for the two founders. Once they decided to start working on the idea, they did not want to waste much time thinking of a name. They had chosen Kimono as the codename for the project based on the phrase 'opening the kimono', which means revealing the inner part of a project or organization to an outside party. For reasons of convenience, the new service was named by the codename. Kimono enables everyone to analyze and collect content on the Internet without detailed technical knowledge. The only thing required is a browser. The company, based in San Francisco, California, pursues the goal of building the best web scraper in existence, replacing the need to write web scrapers entirely and providing a service to users across the world, enabling everyone to build APIs for the "long tail" of the Internet. Today, Kimono is available as a scissors to "cut" small blocks of machine-readable content out of websites. Let's have a look at some key features of Kimono, as well as a few sources of further information.

The Kimono Tool

Name of the tool: Kimono

Operator: Kimonolabs Inc.

Description: Kimono extracts content directly from many websites and makes it available in various formats for further processing. Kimono enables users to design queries for very precise content collection on the Internet, and provides the content in many forms (e.g. XML, RSS etc.). In this way, content can be very precisely captured and prepared for further automated processing.

First launch online: January 2014

URL: https://www.kimonolabs.com

Requirements: Kimono offers a free of charge option with a limited volume of data processing. Usually the volume of data processing within this free plan is sufficient for the average non-commercial user.

Tutorials on the Internet:

- Kimono Documentation

- Kimono Video Tutorials

Examples:

- Moz.com - Using Kimono Labs to Scrape the Web for Free http://moz.com/blog/web-scraping-with-kimono-labs

- scraping.pro - An Independent Review of Kimono Labs Web Scraping Service http://scraping.pro/kimono-labs-review/

Comparable Services:

- Yahoo Dapper http://open.dapper.net

- Feedity (partially fee-based) http://feedity.com

- Feed43 (partially fee-based) http://www.feed43.com

All tutorial and example links can also be found on this book's website at:

www.magaseen.de/MoreValue.html

When using Kimono, please pay attention to the terms of use for any of the websites you are about to use in combination with Kimono, and extract only permissible content. Regardless, please have a look at Kimono's terms of use first.

Content Analysis and Combination

Break Out of the Data Prison

On the evening of February 7, 2007, Tim O'Reilly, founder and CEO of O'Reilly Media, wrote in his blog about *"a milestone in the history of the internet"* (O'Reilly, 2007). What made O'Reilly, known as a technology visionary, publish such an exuberant comment on his website? This comment was triggered by a new Internet service that was presented on the morning of the same day in Sunnyvale, California: Yahoo Pipes.

The transition of the Web of Documents (Web 1.0) into the Web of Content (Web 2.0) was driven by the introduction of many new technologies. One of them was the Real Simple Syndication (RSS) format. With the use of RSS, website providers were able to distribute content similar to a news ticker in a structured form. The resulting continuous flow of content delivered by a website is called a "feed". To access feeds provided by a website, special programs called feed readers are used. Like a magazine subscription, a user can subscribe to a feed on the Internet. After subscribing, the feed takes care of automatically providing a notification, and in many cases, detailed information whenever the content on a website has changed or is updated. The only thing required is that the website a user wants to automatically monitor for content changes offers a feed.

Once subscribed to, a feed continuously provides current information directly derived from the selected website. It is no longer necessary to visit the website manually on a regular basis to discover changes within its content. The feed reader takes care of informing the user automatically, similar to an email program, about any changes on the website. Almost all major websites these days offer an RSS, or the newer format - Atom feed. For example, the New York Times offers feeds on various topics, such as "World News", "US News", and special information from specific editorial departments like "Sports" and "Technology" (NYT RSS feeds). But there is a problem. The individual user can control the content delivered via the feed, but only the provider of a website can determine the specific content that will be distributed by his website's feed. Users can only apply individual filters to the content directly within their personal feed readers. The RSS and Atom feed standard does not provide any functionality to manipulate and change feeds directly by the subscriber. And that is exactly that what was changed with the "milestone" described by Tim O'Reilly. Using Pipes, every user can read, analyze, combine, filter, modify, and publish feeds. The special thing about Pipes is that no comprehensive technical knowledge is required to use the tool. The whole process of designing the individual manipulation of a feed is done graphically. Creating a Pipe requires only the graphical connection of simple pre-defined activities that perform a specific task, like reading an external feed, filtering the content based on a keyword, or substituting a phrase with another. The name Pipes was inspired by the functionality of the UNIX operating system and expresses the stepwise concatenation of activities. Within UNIX-based operating systems, commands can be executed in a linked way, where the output of one command serves as the input to the next, and so on. The result is a chain of commands (a pipe), which is automatically processed by the computer. Yahoo Pipes implements the same principle for the processing of feeds. The service enables every user on the Internet to filter, edit, modify and republish the content of feeds. All of the required processing is performed on the computers of Yahoo. To use this service, all that is required is to create and activate an individual Pipe. After the individually created Pipe is stored, the "new" content is available as a feed on the Internet.

Yahoo Pipes allows the combination and joint processing of multiple feeds based on individually chosen criteria. The results can be exported in various formats, and are thus directly available for further use in other tools. But that is not all. A special functionality of Pipes is that it allows the extraction of content even from websites that offer no feed. Similar to Kimono (discussed in Chapter 4), content can be collected and provided on the Internet for further use and automatic processing, although it has to be said that Kimono offers much easier functionality when it comes to the individual selection and extraction of content on websites.

If Kimono is the tool to create "plastic bricks" based on content derived from the Internet, Pipes is the tool to sort, redesign and re-distribute these "plastic bricks" according to specific criteria. In addition, Pipes can do something that is not possible in the real world of plastic bricks: content from the Internet can be fully manipulated. Manipulation means, in the language of "plastic bricks", converting red blocks with four nubs into blue blocks with eight nubs.

This makes it possible to modify content delivered as a feed in a simple manner. The combination of Kimono and Pipes is the next step towards the realization of the individual Web 3.0.

Although Pipes accepts a few other input formats in addition to RSS and Atom feeds, the emphasis is clearly on these two formats. Over the past several years, many experts have predicted the end of RSS and Atom feeds. Both formats were frequently referred to as out of date, but this prophecy has yet to come true. In fact, quite the contrary. Statistics show that the proliferation and use of feeds has risen slightly in recent years, especially with the top million web pages users frequently visit on the Internet. Feeds have proven to be a stable and popular content distribution technology in the fields of manufacturing, news portals, technology providers, trade, entertainment, social media, sports, and adult entertainment. In fact, an increasing number of websites make their content available as feeds (BuiltWith.com, 2013). Supporting the aim of sharing personalized content on the Web, RSS and Atom feeds are a great help for the average user. Without the functionalities for the collection, combination and automated processing of content from the Internet by combining tools such as Kimono and Pipes, the implementation of the individual Web 3.0 would be much more complicated.

This is especially true when dealing with content scraped from the Internet that contains answers to questions without the need for further analysis, or where only a minor post-processing is required. As far as directly usable content is concerned, usually only the structure of the information delivered must be enhanced for automatic processing. In these cases, there is no need to process the content itself. Examples include airfares on travel portals, address data from an online phone book, the local weather at a meteorological site, the financial data of a company on its website, or an article on a desired topic in a news portal. Content derived from a web page that doesn't provide an answer to a question directly usually requires post-processing before the information is ready for further use. In this case, content is often collected from several sources linked with each other, and the required information is then calculated based on an algorithm. The results often have to be interpreted by humans. If you want to analyze the dependence between the quotes of a company on Twitter and its stock market price, you can collect the required source data directly from the Internet. However, the collected data must be combined and analyzed over a long period of time if sufficient and reliable conclusions are the final goal. Many people think that the collection of raw data on the Internet is complicated and requires programming skills. Tools like Kimono and Pipes simplify this task significantly. In many cases, a solution can even be created without programming at all. The fact that these tools are available for the average user without extensive technical knowledge democratizes the use of the content on the Internet.

Why should only the large stockbroking firms be capable of checking out the suspected causality between Twitter quotes and the stock market price of a company? You should be able to do this on your own for the benefit of your portfolio. If you want to optimize your private investment decisions using this approach, check out the work of Eduardo J. Ruiz and his colleagues from the University of California (Ruiz, Hristidis, Castillo, Gionis, & Jaimes, 2012). Yahoo Pipes is a tool that could help you to gather the necessary data.

Tim O'Reilly rated Pipes so euphorically because he had been waiting for this solution for more than ten years, a solution that allows average users to share content derived from the Internet in a way that was not intended by the original provider of the content without the need to learn programming. For O'Reilly, it was the start of the "programmable" Internet for everyone (O'Reilly, 2007). Yahoo Pipes offered a perspective on the future of the Internet and opened up the door of Timothy Berners-Lee's *"Web of Data"* from a completely new direction. Instead of waiting for the introduction of a universal and standard-based semantic web, Yahoo Pipes presented an easy-to-use tool which allowed every user to extract valuable content on his own, and made it available for further automated use.

The Content Conflict

Within the Web 1.0, content usually could "only" be viewed and not changed by users. Adding individual posts at external websites was almost impossible. To transfer content across multiple websites, either programming skills or a high amount of manual work was required. Anyone who ever tried to copy and paste content from different sources on the Internet knows what I am talking about. By the '90s, due to the high amount of content available on the Internet, this was an almost impossible task. A regular update of manually collected content was completely impossible.

This situation changed with the Web 2.0. For the first time, the "average" user was directly involved in the creating, commenting and changing process of website content. But one limitation remained. In most cases, this new freedom was only granted if the content was edited on the platform of the content provider directly. Take the pure Web 2.0 social network platforms as example. They technically and legally tried to constrain and prevent the use of "their" content outside of their platforms. In contrast, we can - and should - generously deliver our content on proprietary websites, preferably with as much private content as possible. But when we want to use the content stored on the sites, the providers restrict us. Individual links between content stored on different sites spanning the boundaries of different providers are in most cases not possible. Linking the content is often intentionally difficult or impossible. Once we try to make use of content outside of the closed system of a provider, we encounter considerable resistance. And this resistance not only affects the end user, but also affects commercial providers who are in conflict with one another in the Web 2.0 world. A recent example is the withdrawal of the Condé Nast magazines Wired and The New Yorker from the offerings of the social media app Flipboard. Flipboard combines content from various news sources and social networks into an individual digital magazine. The company, founded in Palo Alto, California in 2010, uses RSS formats to collect news content on the Internet and displays it within a truly beautifully designed app. The design has won various awards for its innovative presentation. But since December 2012, Wired and The New Yorker no longer deliver specially adapted content to Flipboard. The reason given for the withdrawal of the magazines' content from the app is a conflict about sharing online advertising revenue. Flipboard requires every content partner to comply with strict rules for displaying advertising and revenue sharing (Indvik, 2012). The withdrawal of Wired and The New Yorker cut off all Flipboard users from especially prepared content of these two magazines. Whoever wants to read Wired or The New Yorker within the Flipboard app in the future is no longer provided with content adjusted for the beautiful layout of the app. Only a reference is made available, instead pointing the user directly to the web pages owned by the magazines. The Flipboard app no longer provides any additional value for the readers of these two magazines. This example perfectly describes how content providers influence the use of "their" content. The efforts to keep content within the Web 2.0 in a closed and controlled system prevent average users from accessing and combining it freely on the Internet. The "owners" of the content try to maintain their control as much as possible. The innovative potential, which could be released by the individual and comprehensive combination of content on the Internet, does not unfold in this way. Due to the fear of losing control, many website providers fence in users, trying to limit their freedom of access and use of Internet content beyond their sphere of influence.

But if content access is granted, fascinating solutions often arise. In this case, the creativity of individual Internet users is released. For example, there is no reason why social business networks cannot be updated individually when it comes to personal data. Why can't we synchronize updates we make on one network directly with another, even within competing networks? The entries on professional social networks are identical in most cases. Most of them cover new skills or job changes. Yet the reduced work required to update personal information on different social networks by central maintenance might not convince everybody of the individual Web 3.0 advantages. Much more obvious are solutions that significantly increase the monetary and non-monetary value users gain by combining the data of different sources. A few companies have recognized the opportunities for new innovative products and services that are concealed therein. KLM Royal Dutch Airlines and the social networks Facebook, LinkedIn and Google+ provide a perfect example of the connection to their individual content. Since the spring of 2012, every member of LinkedIn, Facebook and Google+ has been able to open the personal profile for future fellow travelers when booking a KLM flight. The offering is named "Meet and Seat". Every passenger participating in the program has the opportunity, while selecting a seat, to find out more about the travelers sitting close by. The only prerequisite is granting access to your public Facebook, LinkedIn or Google+ profile. Flying quite often – and in most cases not KLM – I wish my preferred airlines would offer a similar service. Or even better, I could build something like this based on Internet data myself just to plan where I want to sit, or would rather not.

Even though access to airline booking data should not be freely available for everyone, new innovative solutions are possible in many less sensitive areas, solutions that could see the light of day by linking content on the Internet. Why shouldn't we individually link our online calendars with a traffic jam finder that will automatically inform us about potential traffic problems on our way home from a meeting? Or how about updating your calendar automatically, adjusting the start time on the way to a meeting when delays occur? Why shouldn't we set up an assistant to constantly monitor different websites for cheap flight deals to Europe to coincide with a vacation planned in this region for the next summer?

But despite providers actively trying to "protect their content" against the implementation of innovative ideas, the enthusiasm of Tim O'Reilly is quite understandable. As perfect examples, Kimono and Pipes democratized access to the content and the development of individual solutions on the Internet.

No longer can website providers imprison the broader Web 2.0 user base. Extensive technical knowledge is no longer necessary to implement your own individual solution based on the content of the Internet. Since 2007, more and more individual Web 3.0 examples have been implemented using the tools described in this book. Internet users have simplified the search for apartments based on various online listings, including the presentation of results on a digital map. They have created solutions for the automatic distribution of traffic reports, including traffic jam indicators. And they have monitored text messages on popular micro blogging services, and much more. All of these solutions have been built with Yahoo Pipes with almost no programming effort.

It is interesting to note that Yahoo never tried to implement a fee-based service for Pipes. The tool is offered free of charge to this day with full functionality. Let's hope that Yahoo will continue to operate it as a free service for a long time. Without Pipes, many individual Web 3.0 solutions would be unthinkable. Equally interesting, however, is that Pipes never really had a big breakthrough. Nick O'Neill, founder of AllFacebook.com, blamed this on the fact that Pipes is still too complicated for average users and appeared on the market several years too early (O'Neill, 2012). I only agree with the analysis of O'Neill on the second point. Certainly Pipes cannot initially be understood intuitively, but, with some training, even less technically astute users can achieve great results. O'Neill was right in his assumption that Pipes arrived on the market too early. However, his analysis did not go far enough. Too early on the market also means that it must be asked, before which development did it arrive too early? To enable the breakthrough of solutions for the combination and analysis of Internet content such as Pipes, two additional capabilities were missing until recently: the simple automation of processes on the Internet and the possibility of accessing content at any time and at any place. Both are possible today. Let's have a look at some key features of Yahoo Pipes and some sources of further information.

The Yahoo Pipes Tool

Name of the tool: Yahoo Pipes

Operator: Yahoo! Inc.

Description: Yahoo Pipes allows access to content provided via feeds (RSS or Atom feeds), websites, and other structured data sources on the Internet, and the ability to process it in many ways. Content can be filtered, added, modified and combined. Pipes provides a variety of different out of the box modules and functions. The sequential connection of the functionality provided by Pipes allows a user to easily create complex processing steps in a graphical editor. Extensive computer science skills are not required. For example, one can use Pipes to search, filter and combine specific information about a company derived from different RSS feeds collected on various web pages. The resulting set of information can be exported into a single private feed. Pipes reliably provides any new information that appears on one of the observed sites according to freely chosen keywords. Instead of monitoring different sources without any automated help, Pipes will do the job - and continuously without a break!

First launch online: February 2007

URL: http://pipes.yahoo.com/pipes/

Requirements: Pipes is available for free. Only a one-time registration is required. Tip: If you already have a Yahoo account, you can use Pipes with your existing credentials.

Tutorials:

- Learn How to Build a Pipe in Just a Few Minutes
  https://www.youtube.com/watch?v=J3tS_DkmbVA

- Yahoo! Pipes documentation
  http://pipes.yahoo.com/pipes/docs

- Squidoo.com Pipes Guide
  http://www.squidoo.com/yahoo-pipes-guide

- Google Tech Talks Pipes Video
  https://www.youtube.com/watch?v=8XSm8ZyxMrU

Examples:

- Create an RSS feed from any website
  http://www.reaper-x.com/2011/12/27/create-rss-feed-from-any-web-page-using-yahoo-pipes/

- 100 Best Yahoo Pipes Videos
  http://meta-guide.com/videography/100-best-yahoo-pipes-videos/

Comparable Software:

- Huginn (free)
  https://github.com/cantino/huginn

All tutorial and example links can also be found on the website of this book at:

www.magaseen.de/MoreValue.html

When using Pipes, please pay attention to the terms of use for any websites you are about to use in combination with Pipes, and extract only eligible content. In any case, please have a look at Pipes' terms of use first.

Dirk Stähler

The Automated Internet

Let It Work for You

The Internet has become an essential part of our lives. We send e-mails and short messages, write micro-blogs, connect with other people on social networks, create documents and spreadsheets with web-based office software, store digital content like music, pictures or videos in the cloud, have the latest news automatically delivered as feeds, and search for individual information - such as the latest changes in our personal financial portfolio. Before the Internet became popular and so widely used, many of these activities were difficult or completely impossible to realize. Twenty-five years ago we wouldn't have considered the possibilities that have now become reality. But in most cases, we aren't able to make use of the Internet without the help of external service providers. Almost everything we do on the

Internet requires the "help" of a third party, starting with our telephone or cable company and continuing with website providers and data center operators, although it certainly doesn't end there. Our personal computer is more or less "just" the interface to the services provided on the Web.

Taking a closer look at the services we use on the Internet, it is obvious that in many cases, we use different providers for each of the services mentioned above. The reason for this is historical, and can be explained with the development of the Internet over the past several decades. Every Internet service that is popular and market leading these days had a specific focus in its initial phase. Google focused on search, trying to help users find content on the Web. Facebook was focused on building a social network between students at Harvard and other Ivy League Universities. Twitter started off with a publicly available short message service. WhatsApp, the world's most widely used messaging service, positioned itself as an alternative to mobile technology's Short Message Service (SMS). Dropbox started with the simple provision of cloud storage and sharing of files, photos, etc. for private users. This list could be expanded to include several other popular Internet services. Each of these services was able to become the market leader in its niche.

Everyone who has started using services on the Internet in recent years has almost inevitably ended up using the offerings of the respective market leaders at some point. It doesn't matter whether it was e-mail, SMS, social networking, file storage or any another free service provided on the Internet. As a result, today most of us use a variety of different services from different providers. But with the individual growth of service providers comes the effect of expanding their service offerings into new areas. For example – and this is by no means exhaustive – Google developed an online office solution and an e-mail service. Facebook offered a messenger app for smartphones. Twitter identified the potential of their platform for news publishing and slowly developed into a media company (Reißmann, 2012). Until it was bought by Facebook, WhatsApp was trying to become the central communication application on mobile devices. Dropbox has expanded its offerings with specialized solutions for enterprise customers. At some point all of the aforementioned companies started diversifying, trying to gain market share in new areas of business.

Looking at this development, it is not surprising that we can easily recognize an increasing overlap between the service offerings of network companies, website providers, and data center operators intensifying the competition for customers. In addition to comparably young companies like Google, Facebook, or Dropbox, some of whom have been on the market for less than ten years, industry giants are entering the new "business battlefields" as well. Take Microsoft as an example. With Office 360, the guys from Redmond introduced an online office suite and storage, targeting not only Google's offerings, but also their own cash cow MS Office. Apple launched the short message service iMessage, offered online storage with iCloud, and released an online version of its Office software iWorks as well, available on the Internet for free. Even the Deutsche Telekom AG – currently still the majority owner of T-Mobile US Inc. – is trying to gain a share of the market. In addition to traditional telephone and data network services, the German company is expanding its offerings into cloud storage (Telekom Cloud) and the online music business (Music Load). With NSA security concerns in mind, Deutsche Telekom is marketing their offerings with the advantage of supporting the strong German data protection laws, attacking U.S. based cloud providers directly with 25 GB of storage space for free, guaranteed to be on servers in Germany. The only drawback for U.S. customers is that if you want to set up an account, you have to deal with a German language website.

The Winner Doesn't Take It All

Although companies are trying hard to offer more and more integrated solutions under one roof, most end users still prefer a mix of market leaders when it comes to individual solutions. WEB.DE and GMX United Internet are the most commonly used e-mail providers in Germany (Kulka, 2011). Worldwide, it's Google's Gmail service with more than 400 million users (Molla, 2012). In the short message business, the WhatsApp offering is clearly ahead of Apple's iMessage and other offerings (Kuittinen, 2012). When it comes to micro-blogging, Twitter is still the most commonly used service, even though other vendors have made some progress, such Tumblr or Instagram. In the area of social networks, Facebook is still ahead of Google+ and surprisingly, has continued to maintain its leadership even though it is viewed critically by many users and has lost a lot of confidence within its user base (ACSI, 2012). Obviously, Internet-based services gain a high degree of binding force after exceeding a critical mass of users. This effect, clearly visible at Facebook, will stabilize other web-based services for a certain time as well. In the meantime, it is not anticipated that there will be a consolidation of one, or perhaps even several large suppliers. Quite the contrary will be seen. Users are increasingly using different resources when searching for the best services on the Internet. This is especially true in the areas of news, social networking, entertainment, navigation, finance and online shopping (Accenture, 2012).

In addition to the "traditional" use of a PC at home, there is an increasing trend toward accessing specialized content with smartphones and tablets. The average German smartphone user has 24 different apps installed, pulling content from the Internet from each (Google, 2012). In the US, the average is 33 installed apps (Richter, 2013). This is another indicator of the value provided by specialized services and content sources on the Internet.

And there is another advantage that - often unintentionally – is derived from the use of multiple data sources on the Internet: the increased protection of personal data. If your personal data is stored with different providers, it is much harder for them to create comprehensive user profiles. Although this is no guarantee for full data privacy, it provides the average user with an easy opportunity to impede the misuse of personal data. But the disadvantage of such a fragmented Internet service landscape is that content cannot easily be linked in a simple manner. If you are using the Google online calendar, you might like to be automatically reminded on your iPhone or iPad when a deadline approaches without being forced to set up permanent synchronization between Google and your iOS device. This case of use occurs more often than expected. Just think of different Google calendars: a private one, a business related one, a calendar you share with your friends, and so on. Neither Google nor Apple have implemented such functionality out of the box that works on individually specified events. The only synchronization available is "all or nothing".

What is required in general is an easy-to-use and flexible interface that allows combining different content sources on the Internet. An idea as to how this interface could be realized occurred in an unusual location.

Put the Internet to Work - Tools and Content Simply Connected

During the summer of 2010, Linden Tibbets was standing in line at an Indian fast food restaurant in San Francisco. But instead of focusing on the menu, his thoughts revolved around a problem within a software project he was working on. A problem he wanted to solve by using event-driven programming (Tibbets, 2010). Event-driven programming enables computers to respond flexibly to changes that occur during the execution of a program. There is no longer a need to specify the exact flow of a program in advance. Within an event-driven program, only events that must be reacted to and their related program steps are defined, regardless of when and in what order they occur. The concept is simple: when certain conditions occur during the execution of a program, the software responds with a defined behavior, described simply as the IF-THEN rule. IF a defined event occurs, THEN a specific part of the program – an action – is executed. If a user makes certain inputs, or sensors report a change of conditions, the program responds with a behavior associated with the event.

While Linden was waiting in the queue at the fast food restaurant, he came up with the idea to connect services available on the Internet, such as email, online calendars, social networks and so on, with a similar principle. Events occurring within a service on the Internet should trigger actions at other services. Linden was convinced that the benefit of services provided on the Internet could be significantly increased by individually linking many of these services together. It was his belief that the creativity of many people, experimenting freely with connecting services on the Web, would result in new solutions, some not even anticipated (Tibbets, 2010). This idea was so appealing to him that he started to work on this web-based service with his friend Jesse Tane. In

December 2010, the result was presented to the public: IFTTT. The name is an abbreviation for IF This Then That = IFTTT.

IFTTT enables everyone to connect independent services on the Internet with a simple relationship. With an easy to understand IF-THEN-link, many well-known web applications can be coupled. If an event occurs within a triggering service, an action is activated within a target service. For example, setting up an individualized notification on Apple's iPhone or iPad based on an event triggered by Google's online calendar can now be implemented on a case-by-case basis without technical knowledge, and without connecting the two services directly. With IFTTT, you don't have to synchronize a Google calendar with the iPhone or iPad. The only thing required is a service that sends an alert to your mobile device whenever the triggering event on Google Calendar occurs. For this service, IFTTT offers a connection with the Internet-based Pushover notification service. To automate the entire process, you only have to create an account with Pushover (https://pushover.net) and download the one-time fee-based software for the iPhone or iPad at a price of $4.49 (as of 6/27/2014). The software is available for Android users as well, in case they do not want to directly link their smartphone calendar with Google's.

Compared with other individual Web 3.0 solutions, such as Kimono and Pipes, IFTTT is much easier for the average user. This is possible because within IFTTT, a user can only use predefined links for the connection to different Internet-based services. For the time being, users of IFTTT cannot integrate new web-based services into the tool by themselves. Setting up your own extensions is not possible. It is also impossible to extend the actions triggered by IFTTT, and the manipulation of the content exchanged between services is limited. Nevertheless, it is amazing what can be achieved with IFTTT. Today, IFTTT provides hundreds of connection capabilities with a simple mouse click that until recently required extensive programming.

Linden Tibbets called the flexible connection of web-based services using IFTTT a "digital duct tape". In fact, this analogy is perfect. IFTTT enables the individual connection between several Internet services, connections that weren't initially planned by their providers. But at the same time, Tibbets pointed out the limitations of IFTTT. In his blog he wrote: *"I realize that IFTTT only addresses a small subset of the ways in which you can be creative with digital information, but within that subset there are tons of opportunities to hook together existing services, devices and objects"* (Tibbets, 2010). However, he assumes that by using the available service connections alone, tasks can be automated in a way that no one had thought of before. Currently, IFTTT offers connections for 124 popular Web services, called channels. This includes interfaces with Google Calendar, Twitter, Facebook, Dropbox or LinkedIn. Whatever combinations of services provided are used are limited only by the creativity of the individual user. For example, you can send a notification to a cell phone when a particular product at a specific price appears on Craigslist, turn the light on at home with a simple email, have your neighbor's phone called with a predefined message when a package delivery is scheduled and you are not at home (to alert your neighbor that the package might be dropped at his house), or – my favorite – set up a "meeting rescue call" for your own cell phone you can trigger by a simple iMessage (your phone will ring and you can sneak out with a good excuse). And the best thing is, IFTTT's service is free.

But the real power of IFTTT becomes obvious when it is combined with Kimono and Pipes. With this combination, it is possible to include content from the Internet where there is no native IFTTT channel available. Particularly important for this use case is the previously mentioned RSS format. Kimono and Pipes are capable of generating customized RSS feeds based on data collected, analyzed, processed and combined with these tools. Passed to IFTTT, it is easy to automate a lot of different actions based on the variety of content provided by Kimono and Pipes. This gives rise to solutions that were unthinkable for the average Internet user until just recently.

With the combination of Kimono, Pipes and IFTTT, you can collect individually selected forum postings – even from websites that don't provide RSS feeds or IFTTT connections – and place in cloud storage for later analysis. You can keep track of who wrote what on any subject on the Internet, monitor your digital shadow to find out if someone publishes something you should know, and a lot of other things. The possibilities are only limited by your own ideas of content combination. The connected use of Kimono, Pipes and IFTTT point out the mighty possibilities that will be available for the average Internet user in the very near future.

As Timothy Berners-Lee pointed out in 2001: *"The real power of the Semantic Web will be realized when people create many programs that collect Web content from diverse sources, process the information, and exchange the results with other programs. The effectiveness of such software agents will increase exponentially as more machine-readable Web content and automated services become available"* (Berners-Lee et al., 2001).

When Berners-Lee wrote this in a Scientific American magazine article, he still believed that the implementation of this vision would require the generation of standardized machine-readable content. It turned out that the solutions available today work differently. They are focused on providing simple interfaces connecting frequently used Web services and leaving the rest of the content preparation work and individual service linking to each user. The set up of a uniform structure defining how content on the Internet must be prepared for machine readability and comprehensive data exchange capability - for example, RDF or WOL - is in many cases no longer necessary. These days, the flexible and individual connection to content is important. Users of the digital "scissors", "plastic bricks" and "duct tape" link content from all over the Internet with just little technical knowledge. Generally accepted standards for machine-readable content preparation are no longer needed. Every individual user carries out the necessary adjustments to the structure and content. Of course, the featured services only provide basic functionalities for the collection and manipulation of content and the automation of activities on the Internet. But in many cases, this is quite sufficient as long as users are in control of the content. The only challenge for the users of these combined services is to identify valuable content on the Internet, and make sure that the information derived from this content is delivered at the right time. Having already explained tools that allow one to collect and manipulate content and automate activities based on Internet services, there is only one last thing missing to assure delivery right on time. For the development of a ubiquitous individual Web 3.0, we need mobile computing power. But before we dive into that topic, let's have a look at some key features of IFTTT and some sources of further information.

The IFTTT Tool

Name of the tool: IFTTT

Operator: IFTTT

Description: IFTTT provides functionality that interconnects a variety of popular web services that were not initially intended to be connected by their providers, and automates the interactions between these services. IFTTT offers interfaces for many web services in the areas of social networking, news, cloud storage, entertainment, home automation, self-monitoring, and much more. A simple IF-THIS-THEN-THAT relation creates links between these services. IFTTT guides the average user through the system with a simple and understandable dialogue. Two web services can be simultaneously linked together. Currently, IFTTT offers 112 different web service interfaces. For example, with IFTTT, it is possible to monitor whether the Internet radio Last.fm offers free music downloads as soon as new music emerges. When that music is available, IFTTT instantly creates a copy of its mp3 file in your Dropbox. And with a second IFTTT task, you can have your Dropbox inform you automatically as soon as new music arrives by SMS, iMessage, e-mail or a phone call. Every task created within IFTTT - called a Recipe - is automatically updated every 15 minutes. As soon as new content is available, it triggers the service and a predefined action is executed.

First launch online: December 2010

URL: https://ifttt.com

Requirements: IFTTT is free of charge. Only a one-time registration is required.

Tutorials:

*   Snazzy Labs - IFTTT tutorial on YouTube
    http://www.youtube.com/watch?v=cAb
    B6qmTFU4

*   Matthew Woodward - Save Time with IFTTT
    http://www.matthewwoodward.co.uk/ti
    ps/how-to-use-ifttt-to-save-time-
    automate-a-behind-the-scenes-look/

*   The IFTTT Guide of the University of Wy-
    oming
    http://www.wyomingextension.org/wiki
    /index.php5?title=Learning_Guide:IFTTT

Examples:

- 1st Webdesigner 20 Cool IFTTT Recipes
  http://www.1stwebdesigner.com/design
  /20-ifttt-recipes-automate-online-
  activities/

- 10 IFTTT Recipes to Optimize Your Business
  http://mashable.com/2013/03/28/ifttt-
  recipes-business/

Comparable services:

- Zapier (partially fee-based)
  https://zapier.com

- Wappwolf (partially fee-based)
  http://wappwolf.com

All tutorial and example links can also be found
on this book's website at:

www.magaseen.de/MoreValue.html

When using IFTTT, please pay attention to the
terms of use of any websites you are about to use
in combination with IFTTT. In any case, please
have a look at IFTTT terms of use first.

Dirk Stähler

Everything is Mobile

Changes in the Way We Access Content

Winter 2009/2010: There were rumors and speculation within the computer manufacturer and IT community for weeks that revolved around the question of what groundbreaking product Apple was about to reveal in the upcoming weeks. Well-informed sources reported that it would be the first practical implementation of a tablet, a device positioned somewhere between a smartphone and a laptop. Martin Peers summed up the excitement around Apple's new product on December 30, 2009 in the Wall Street Journal in a single sentence that explained it perfectly:

The last time there was this much excitement about a tablet, it had some commandments written on it. (Peers, 2009)

When Steve Jobs introduced the new device on January 27th at the Moscone Convention Center in San Francisco, he opened his presentation with the words that he was about to present a *"revolutionary and magical device"* that comprises a completely new experience for mobile Internet access (Apple Inc., 2010). The name of the new product: iPad.

Contrary to the previous excitement, reactions varied from initially reluctant to extremely negative. They ranged from "let's wait and see how potential users will react" to "a product nobody needs". However, most analysts agreed on one major point: in the near future, there was no great success predicted for the iPad. Marisa Taylor summed up the negative reviews of "leading" bloggers from well-known news portals like Gizmodo, PC World, CNN and others. The criticism ranged from a lack of multi-tasking, the blockage of multi-media content based on Flash, the limiting Apple "ecosystem" imprisoning users, and did not stop with the complaints about the unhandy size of the device (Taylor, 2010).

Particularly negative comments came from Adam Frucci, a blogger at the technology and gadget website Gizmodo. He listed the negative features of the iPad in detail. In addition to the limitations already mentioned, he extended the list by including: the lack of a camera, the ugly keyboard, the non-existent HDMI output and the need to buy additional adapters for every device you wanted to connect with the iPad. "It has some absolutely backbreaking failures that will make buying one the last thing I would want to do", said Frucci (Frucci, 2010). One of the few who commented prudently was David Pogue in his blog for the New York Times:

Like the iPhone, the iPad is really a vessel, a tool, a 1.5-pound sack of potential. It may become many things. It may change an industry or two, or it may not. It may introduce a new category - something between phone and laptop - or it may not. And anyone who claims to know what will happen will wind up looking like a fool. (Pogue, 2010)

He recommended that we should first wait and see how the new device category would develop. With this advice, he was absolutely right. By October 2010, the situation had been settled in favor of the iPad. Apple sold 3.3 million units in the first three months. Business customers and consumers started to reconsider buying PCs, and deliberated purchasing tablets instead (Robertson, 2010). In October 2012, Apple announced yet another record. Only two and a half years after the introduction of the iPad, more than 100 million units had been sold. In the second quarter of 2012, Apple sold more iPads than any other manufacturer sold PCs (Lawler, 2012). Contrary to the criticisms initially expressed, the new device had created and established a completely new market at an unbelievable pace. It created the market for portable tablet computers. Steve Jobs succeeded where other giants of the computer industry had failed. Just think about Microsoft's attempt to introduce a windows-based tablet computer. Hardly anyone wanted to buy the unwieldy device, which was difficult to use with a pen. Its market success failed to materialize, and the device was abandoned. Apple, however, achieved a breakthrough with the iPad in a short time.

If you are travelling through airports worldwide today, you can clearly see the change that has taken place. Tablets have prevailed. Pay attention to them on your next flight. When standing in line at the security checkpoint, while waiting for boarding, and on the plane itself, you will find more people with a tablet than a laptop. Many have exchanged the laptop for a tablet, although these small devices are actually less powerful than a laptop. The reason for this is that tablets – especially the category of tablets first created by Apple – allow a hitherto unknown freedom in accessing the Internet. Connected with the Internet, tablet performance restrictions are more than compensated for by accessing the computing resources available somewhere on the net. However, the required Internet access also creates a dependency. A tablet without it is only partially usable.

But the tablet is not the only device that is challenging the supremacy of the PC. A second group of mobile devices is growing more and more popular as well: smartphones. Among mobile phones, their share rose in Germany between 2011 and 2012 by more than 60 percent (Google, 2012). Taken together, 44 percent of all mobile phones in the European Union countries of Spain, Italy, France, the UK and Germany in 2011 were smartphones (ComScore, 2012). A total of 70 percent of Internet page views in Germany originate from tablets and smartphones (Interrogare, 2012). This development is also reflected globally. In the U.S. the number of smartphone users grew by more than 160% between 2010 and 2014, up to a total of 164 million users (statista, 2014). The global market for tablets has been growing by more than 75 percent per year for some time (IDC, 2013).

Mobile devices are displacing the conventional computer. They are the first generation of device that is capable of accessing content on the Internet anywhere and anytime. Michael Saylor explained the success of smartphones and tablets with the simple control concept first introduced with multi-touch displays, providing even less experienced users an intuitive operation, affordable applications (apps), and a new class of product distribution system via app stores. Tablets and smartphones are definitely the cheapest computers with the cheapest applications that have ever existed. The required hard- and software was never available at such low prices, compared on the basis of performance, and was never accessible by such an unprecedented number of users as it is today. With the expansion of faster wireless networks and lower flat-rate fees, a completely new use of the Internet has become possible. For the first time in the history of mankind, the knowledge of the world is easily accessible to the masses (Saylor, 2012), and the potential is far from being exhausted. Today, 70 percent of the world's population owns a basic mobile phone. It's only a matter of time before the majority of them will switch to web-enabled mobile devices. Today, content is quite often accessed on the Internet via mobile devices and apps. According to Flurry, a company specialized in the evaluation of mobile devices and services, each smartphone or tablet user spends an average of one and a half hours per day with small programs on mobile devices. In contrast, the use of the classic Web browser on PCs has declined (Newark-French, 2012). You've probably observed this development on your own. In many cases, it is much easier and more enjoyable accessing Internet content via smartphones or tablets using specialized apps, compared with a web browser on a PC or laptop. These specialized programs are usually more convenient to operate and provide better-prepared results for the smaller screens of smartphones and tablets. Even websites specially customized for mobile devices often cannot compete with mobile apps in terms of ease of use.

However, the concept of specialized apps for smartphones and tablets has a significant disadvantage. Often, it is impossible for the user to control the sources from which an app draws and receives its content. Therefore, it often remains unclear whether the creator or provider of an app ignored particularly useful content. In many cases, there is no way for the average user to make individual adjustments or additions to the content sources used by an app. Take gas price comparison apps – in some countries very popular due to high energy prices – as an example. As the data is collected from a crowdsourced base, drivers deliver actual gas prices at the pump to multiple app providers. In comparison, if you are using just one of the apps, you have to trust that it provides the best and most up to date content for gas stations at your location. Statistically, the chance of getting the most accurate data would be much higher if the data were provided by multiple sources. In terms of apps, that would mean querying the data from multiple gas comparison apps before choosing a gas station. But unfortunately it is not possible to get fuel prices from different app providers in a single app. If gas prices, as reported by drivers within various apps, could be combined, the quality of the results would improve. This effect would occur within many cases of content-based analyses in the app world. It would be extremely helpful if users could toggle between different data sources and combine the results within one app, giving them freedom to add new data sources and additional content whenever they need it. In addition, in most cases apps cannot be linked, and do not allow the easy exchange and sharing of content. Only when developers have devised an exchange in advance is it possible to transfer data between different apps. Of course, when linking data from different sources, copyright problems arise in addition to the technical problems (more on copyright issues in the next chapter). That's the main reason why an app provider usually doesn't offer this functionality, and an individual combination of different apps is often not possible.

This limitation is partly reinforced by built-in restrictions in the operating systems used in modern smartphones and tablets. Take Apple iOS devices as an example. The iOS operating system, used in every iPhone, iPad and iPod, limits the ability to share data between apps. With its iOS 8, Apple begins to open up the system a bit, allowing apps to communicate a little better.

The Problem with Apps

The concept of small, easy to install apps for mobile devices has - as impressive as it is - two serious problems. The first problem is that users usually do not have any influence on which data sources are used by an app. In almost every case, it is difficult to add your own content sources, or to use content not intended for access. This is a limitation that is based on the internal behavior of the single app on a mobile device. Therefore, I call it an "internal app problem". The second problem is that often a user cannot create the necessary connections to exchange content between apps. The functionality necessary to exchange content between apps on a flexible and easy to set-up basis often does not exist at all. This is a limitation that is based on the external behavior of apps, limiting the capability to exchange data between apps on a mobile device. Therefore, I call it an "external app problem".

Both deficiencies are the initial reasons for a change: adding a new flexible interface concept to the manner in which mobile applications on smartphones and tablets will be created in the future. The forces behind this change are very similar to those that triggered the transition from Internet portals to search engines at the beginning of the last decade. Until 2000, Yahoo was the undisputed market leader in Internet portals. Most people "searching" for information on the Internet during this time went to Yahoo for help first. The portal, initially created as a list of interesting websites by postgraduate students Jerry Yang and David Filo for their own use at Stanford University, established itself as a central entry point for people browsing the Internet by the end of the 1990s. The hierarchical table of contents of the World Wide Web provided by Yahoo proved to be ideal for both experienced and new users of the Internet during the early days. The catalog-like structure initially allowed organizing content on the Internet in an easily readable and clearly arranged manner. But with growing experience, the picture changed. More and more users left the "phase of exploration of the web" and entered the "phase of expectation from the net". The questions changed from *"what is out there to discover"* to *"I want to find something that I know is there"* (author's note: just not exactly where) (Battelle, 2005). This dramatically changed the way in which users searched for content on the Internet.

There was a shift from editorially compiled directories to word-like searches. The main beneficiary of this change was – at that time – a small company based in Mountain View California, called Google. The main initiator of this change was the growing user experience. When Yahoo's rise began with its portal, most users did not know what was out there on the Internet. Initially, a list of the content in the form of a directory was therefore extremely helpful. But the need for such a list was reduced with the increased knowledge of the user. Around the turn of the millennium, the network had grown so widely that most users were confident that specific information meeting their needs would definitely be out there somewhere. The question was no longer "does it exist", but rather "how can I find it". Google's approach of a term-based query entered into a simple search field was superior compared with the editorially maintained directories (Battelle, 2005). We are about to partially experience the same effect in the mobile app environment: moving away from pre-selected content, that is, content selected by app developers. To put it another way, it is moving away from fixed application scopes towards flexible and individual combinations of use-cases. In the future, we will use flexible interfaces so that content can be used within other applications where appropriate. How these mobile device solutions may look in the future can be seen today at "Yahoo Pipes for the iPhone", or the "KimonoApp" functionality. Both solutions enable every user to create individual content-based apps optimized for the small screens of mobile devices. Another example of the new generation of connected apps is provided by IFTTT. Published on July 10, 2013, the app "IFTTT for iPhone" is the mobile version of the "electronic duct tape" discussed in an earlier chapter. And last but not least, Apple's efforts to make iOS 8 a little more open for data exchange between apps is an indication that some of the industry giants are slowly beginning to understand. And now – just for a second – imagine the power that could be set free by combining these apps into one superior solution. Such functionality in the hands of every average user will, however, create some resistance – the resistance of those who think they own the content.

The Big Guys Strike Back

Forced to Share?

"We're moving to a culture and economy based on access rather than ownership – for that sharing and partnerships are essential", noted Lisa Gansky in an interview in the magazine BizTechDay (Yeung, 2010).

For centuries, many successful business ventures have been based on the principle of sharing, initially focusing on long living assets based on the notions of renting and using only as needed, instead of buying and owning them. Classic examples for these kinds of business models are hotel beds, energy supply infrastructure, or entertainment and leisure activities, such as movies, concerts or theater plays. Only extremely wealthy people came up with the idea of buying apartments in several remote locations, merely based

on the possibility of wanting to live there some-
day for some time. Renting a hotel room is much
cheaper. The same is true for the energy infrastructure. Shared resources for energy production
and distribution ensure a supply at a low cost for
a large number of people. Most obvious is the
principle of sharing within the entertainment industry. Whether one person or hundreds attend a
concert, the listening experience is basically the
same for everyone. It is shared, apart from limitations of space and audio quality when there is a
very high number of concertgoers.

Today, more and more business models are being
turned upside down by the principle of sharing.
This first became obvious in the case of products
that could be easily digitized, such as music. Digitized music has been easily shared since the
1990s without great effort – in most cases illegal-
ly. The music industry was the first major victim
of digital file sharing platforms such as Napster.
Currently, the film industry loses content on a
large scale due to piracy. And the next industry
has already been targeted. The print business is
facing serious challenges that will further increase in number in the upcoming years. New
means of accessing physical and digital publica-
tions will change this media landscape soon. The
old business models based on physical distribution of printed products no longer work. But
that's not enough. Even industries that seem to be

immune and stable at first glance when it comes to sharing have been severely affected, especially industries that offer durable goods at a high price not attractive enough to be purchased and owned by the individual consumer – or user to be more precise – on a regular basis. The company Zipcar has proven, for example, that the principle of sharing can be implemented in the business of individual mobility. The company's car sharing services, offered in several North American cities, are fully supported digitally. With a smartphone, members can easily find an available car nearby, book it, unlock it and even start the engine. The idea was so successful that the company was taken over by the Avis Budget Group for approximately $500 million in March 2013. Another business that is beginning to warm up to the idea of sharing is the fashion industry. The company Girl Meets Dress.com offers exclusive women's designer clothing for rental. Whether for a wedding, graduation party, ball or whatever event you can imagine that requires formal attire that isn't part of your wardrobe, it is no longer necessary to purchase a designer piece. For a single use, it can easily be rented. This business idea only became possible with the help of the Internet, which provided enabling technologies to easily handle individual requests on a large scale in an uncomplicated manner. Besides this special offer for women, there is something for men that could be shared via the Internet as well. Take the North

Portland Tool Library as an example, where all kinds of tools are offered for rent, ranging from carpentry, woodworking and gardening tools, to electrical equipment of any kind.

Besides goods that can be shared, an essential requirement for this change in business models is the ability to share information. Offers like Zipcar, Girls Meets Dress.com, or The North Portland Tool Library couldn't be implemented economically without the help of modern information technology and the Internet. The main reason for this change is based on a commodity, one not easily sharable on a large scale until a few years ago and added by the Internet: content! The Internet accelerated a fundamentally new approach of producing and selling goods that differs from traditional business models. Through shared use, consumers can obtain a greater variety of goods and can choose from a broader spectrum offered. All of this is based on the shared use of products, services and information (Gansky, 2010). With the Internet, we are capable of easily locating, copying and sharing digital content. The only prerequisite is free and unlimited access to information.

An example of how this access can be organized in an extremely open manner is the Open Data movement. This movement has set for itself the task of making content from government agencies and the public administration freely accessible for every interested citizen. This includes, with no claim for completeness, spatial data, official statistics, traffic information and research results. The collection and compilation of these data sets is often financed with tax money, so there is a reasonable interest in making it publicly available. It stands to reason, then, to provide access to this data for a broader public use for free. The idea is that when made accessible to a wide range of users, new business ideas and values are created based on open data. Worldwide, more and more governments are participating in the Open Data movement. Canada, the USA, England, Finland, Estonia and Denmark have all introduced internationally acclaimed programs promoting free access to public data (Hammell, Perricos, Branch, & Lewis, 2011). The European Commission estimates the economic potential of open data derived from public administration sources at up to around 40 billion euros per year. For this reason even the German government, in the past rather hesitant, wants to promote the open data movement. The goal is to enable new applications and services that create added value for citizens, government, science and business. A centrally accessible open government platform was planned for the end of 2013 by the German government (Klessmann, Denker, Schieferdecker, & Schulz, 2012). Unfortunately, the implementation of solutions for the user-friendly access to public data is still in its infancy within the German administration. There is no recognizable visible interest within the German administration to share their content with external parties. A sign of resistance is reflected by the change of the program's name. Originally launched under the label "Open Government Data Platform", the project had been renamed to govdata.de, a clearer indication from the perspective of the administration staff who really "own the data". Data collected with tax money is still regarded as the property of governments and public administrations (Matzat, 2013). It is for these reasons that the program never got off of the ground.

Free access to content on the Internet is not welcome everywhere. Besides public authorities and government administrations, private companies are trying to increase the protection of their content as well. A particularly clear example of how entire industries are trying to defend themselves against the exploitation of their content is the German legislative initiative for an ancillary copyright law, which is massively supported by local publishers. It aims to prohibit the commercial use of even the smallest excerpts from newspapers and magazines. If it would have been adopted in its original draft, search engines would no longer have been allowed to display even the smallest extracts of text derived from other websites for free. Google was one of the companies that responded to this attack on its core business. With the campaign *"Defend your network, get involved"*, the company tried to gain influence on the German legislative process and weaken the bill. Stefan Tweraser, country manager at Google Germany, argued in December 2012 that an ancillary copyright law would mean less information for consumers and higher costs for businesses (Reinbold, 2012). But not only search engine providers, led by financial interests, raised concerns. The Max Planck Society, an independent non-governmental and non-profit association of German research institutes named in honor of its former president, theoretical physicist Max Planck, examined the negative impact of the proposed law within its Department for Intellectual Property and Competition Law. The institute came to the conclusion that access to external content could be easily obstructed by technical restrictions. However, many content providers do not make use of these technologies to restrict access. Content owners obviously have an interest in sharing their intellectual property to increase their visibility on the Internet. Furthermore, the Max Planck Society pointed out that the law would be primarily used to generate license revenue at major digital content providers and creators. Smaller commercial providers who depend on third-party content to offer their services would be forced to pass along the additional expense of licensing to their customers, making their products and services more expensive and less attractive to consumers. The Max Planck Society concluded that the draft of the ancillary copyright law was not thought through and would have a negative impact on the economy and public (Max-Planck-Institut für Immaterialgüter- und Wettbewerbsrecht, 2012). In June 2010, the draft of the bill was unanimously rejected during a hearing at the German Federal Ministry of Justice. Nevertheless, the legislative initiative was passed, showing how successful German publishers are able to intensify their political lobbying despite the fact that scientists warned of the negative consequences. After the Bundestag and Bundesrat – the two German legislative authorities – had approved the bill, it became effective on August 1, 2013. A slight amendment, made shortly before the bill was passed, added a passage that *"single words or small snippets of text"* are excluded from the ancillary copyright. It is easy to anticipate that this fuzzy definition is about to tie up the courts in the near future because the legislature failed to define what is meant by a "small snippet of text". Small commercial Internet providers will be deterred from accessing third party content in the future. It will block new and innovative product and service offerings in the digital world. This affects all users on the Internet. Even Timothy Berners-Lee's vision of a semantic web, which arises when people begin to build software agents that collect content from diverse sources, process it and exchange information with other software, is affected by the new intellectual law, at least on a commercial level. If the commercial access of third party content is restricted by law, the more important it becomes to enable every individual – on a non-commercial basis – to make use of the content on the Internet without deep technical know-how. Private access to content on the Internet can be considered as the practical implementation of Article 5 of the German Constitution. Based on Article 5, every German citizen has the right to inform himself freely using every publicly accessible source. In my opinion, every German citizen should therefore be allowed to use publicly accessible content on the Internet for private purposes. Something similar exists in the U.S. with the First Amendment to the United States Constitution, where it says that *"Congress shall make no law respecting an establishment of religion, or prohibiting the free exercise thereof; or abridging the freedom of speech, or of the press; or the right of the people peaceably to assemble, and to petition the Government for a redress of grievances"*.

The current discussion about the new intellectual property law made it pretty clear that the content on the Internet has real commercial value. It is understandable that companies want to gain or maintain control over it. In addition to publishers, this also includes major Internet companies.

And while considering the large Internet companies, an interesting paradox becomes visible. Having aggressively fought against the ancillary copyright bill, they now exhibit completely different behavior when "their own" data, provided by their users, moves into focus. In this case, free access is no longer desired.

Look at Facebook, for example. The company claims the right to use, using its own discretion, all images and video content that has ever been published by a user in connection with the use of the social network. The right will remain effective as long as the user does not delete the content. But there is even more. When content is shared with other Facebook users – the main purpose of a social network and what happens with most of the content – Facebook reserves the right to continue using this content until the last user deletes it (Facebook, 2013). However, free access is limited when Facebook's "own content" is affected. Within its terms of use it says:

"You will not collect users' content or information, or otherwise access Facebook, using automated means (such as harvesting bots, robots, spiders, or scrapers) without our prior permission." (Facebook, 2013)

Even Google, very actively involved in advocating "free access" during the dispute over the German Ancillary Copyright Bill, reacts sensitively when it comes to providing access to its "own data". In the terms of use it says:

"Don't interfere with our Services or try to access them using a method other than the interface and the instructions that we provide." (Google, 2014a)

At first glance, this limitation is not surprising. Every provider on the Internet has the unrestricted right to define how its services – in the case of Google, mainly content – is to be used. However, upon further reading of the terms of use, an irritation occurs. One of the following paragraphs states, among other things:

"You retain ownership of any intellectual property rights that you hold in that content. In short, what belongs to you stays yours." (Google, 2014a)

If it is really mine, I should be allowed to access it with any method I desire. The company also produces comprehensive profiles of its users. In addition to personal data, Google "may" process device-related information, log data, location-based information, unique application numbers, and much more according to their own privacy statements, information that could be used to provide targeted advertising (Google, 2014b).

Taking a closer look, the boundaries between supporters and opponents of freely accessible content on the Internet becomes blurred even further. Publishers are fighting against the exploitation of their content by search engines, but also depend on Google and others to refer to them in search results. Still, they invest heavily in the improvement of search results positioned on "enemy" search engines because only results that are present within the first result pages of a search can expect enough visitor traffic on their own pages to generate substantial advertising revenue. Almost all major publishers still depend on this model to finance their online offerings. Only the New York Times has managed to establish an alternative source of online income by implementing a paywall for accessing more than 10 articles online per month. Many New York Times customers understand that $15 per month is not too much for quality journalism. All other major newspapers on the globe are still experimenting with new approaches on how to make money in the digital world, and it is by no means certain whether a general portable financing concept for the adaptation of traditional publishers will ever exist. Maybe in the near future, a previously unknown player will show up and kill all of the established traditional print businesses. The purchase of the Washington Post by Amazon founder Jeff Bezos is perhaps the first step in that direction.

On the other hand, the opposition to the German Ancillary Copyright Bill continues the effort to restrict the use of "their" content by third parties wherever possible. No sign of openness. The activities range from unspecified announcements leading to anticipatory obedience and technical limitations, up to open legal defense.

Attack on Innovations

Two examples illustrate how small and innovative companies are pressured. In June 2007, the San Diego based Startup Listpic ran into a conflict with the much bigger online classifieds portal Craigslist.org. Listpic had developed a website that scraped images right from Craigslist's digital marketplace and displayed the content in a compelling form, making it much easier for users to browse entries by images, instead of the text-based format of the original page. The solution improved the navigation and overview within Craigslist's content. The content was presented on Listpic's own web pages, but users were always referred back to the original Craigslist page when they showed an interest in buying. So no purchasing traffic was taken away from Craigslist. Nevertheless, according to Jim Buckmaster, CEO of Craigslist.org at that time, the solution violated the terms of use of the online classifieds portal. Within one day, Craigslist's website was technically altered, preventing Listpic from scraping content, and due to this modification, Listpic no longer worked (McHugh, 2007). The penalty for using Listpic's technology with Craigslist's content was that this innovative and extremely user-friendly idea was destroyed. Today, Listpic operates under the name PicClick (www.picclick.com), and offers a similar service based on eBay content. For Craigslist's portal, this user-friendly and clearly laid out presentation of content is no longer available, resulting in a consumer experience that is less pleasant and useful than it could have been.

IFTTT recently experienced how established Internet companies try to actively influence their offers. In August 2012, Michael Sippey, Vice-President of Twitter, announced changes within Twitter's third-party developer rules, altering the way they could access the service (Sippey, 2012). In essence, Twitter wanted to gain tighter control over the ways external parties could access its content. Along with the new requirements, Twitter also announced that the new rules would be restrictively imposed in the future. Up to that point, Twitter did not restrictively monitor its existing guidelines. The new rules included, among other things, restrictions about the transfer of tweets – a name for the short message content published on Twitter – from Twitter to other applications. It is for exactly this purpose that IFTTT had a frequently used service in place. Based on this service, tweets could be searched for keywords and forwarded to a variety of other services on the Internet. For example, with just a few clicks, you could easily set-up an agent that monitored tweets of certain individuals or organizations and automatically triggered actions on the Internet when certain keywords were found within the content, a simple form of Twitter monitoring that even users with no technical knowledge could set up in minutes. But with the new guidelines, Twitter started to shatter these innovative solutions. And the pressure created achieved the desired results. On Tuesday, September 20, 2012, IFTTT founder Linden Tibbets informed users by email that the controversial function would be deactivated by the end of the month (IFTTT, 2012). It is not clear whether Twitter pressured the management of IFTTT directly or the company acted in anticipatory obedience.

One thing is clear, however. The concerns expressed by the Max Planck Society are not a bleak vision of the future. They are reality.

At first glance, the balance of power appears to be clear. Considering influencing the business models of innovative startups seems to be both technically and legally easy, and large service providers appear to have a significant advantage over small startups. Does this mean that the question "who will win the content race" has already been answered? A closer look reveals a more nuanced picture though. When it comes to the commercial use of third party content on the Internet, it is important to distinguish between two types of enterprise business models: content services and infrastructure services.

Content services create a specific product for the end user based on external content accumulated from other websites. An example of this group of companies was Listpic, whose product was based on images (content) from Craigslist. These types of companies always face the problem that they are critically dependent on content from external sources. If access to this external content is blocked, it will destroy their business model quickly, as seen with Listpic's model, torn asunder within just one day. This type of company is always at risk, easily pressured legally or technically by the actual source of the content, proving a deterrent to investors. Finding someone willing to finance startups in the content service business that depends on third party content is extremely hard because it is generally risky. There is almost no way to guarantee that the third parties they depend on will not destroy the business model.

On the other hand, there are infrastructure services. Companies following this kind of business model provide the infrastructure for collecting, analyzing, processing and storing content on the Internet. Unlike content service providers who deal directly with the content scraped from the Internet itself, they only provide the tools for these tasks. It is left to the individual user to use the content accessed from the Internet with the tools they provide. Examples of these kinds of services include Kimono, Pipes and IFTTT. It is difficult, even though it can be done, for the "suppliers" of content to block every individual solution created using these tools because there are so many of them. The result is a variety of individual solutions that make use of the Internet's content. And not all of them can be controlled. For example, the combination of Yahoo Pipes and IFTTT initially allowed bypassing the restriction Twitter enforced on IFTTT. Combining a Yahoo Pipes search within tweets and forwarding the results via RSS to IFTTT could easily replicate the deprecated functionality. But since Twitter fully implemented the technical API changes announced in June 2013, this trick stopped working. But the Internet community reacted quickly, and just a few days later, tools emerged on the Internet that allowed the rebuilding of this functionality. Ian Gray presented a solution on how Twitter content can still be read and distributed via RSS (Gray, 2013). It is somewhat more difficult to implement than the original "detour" service offered by IFTTT and Yahoo Pipes, but not an insurmountable obstacle, even for less technically skilled users. This example shows how difficult it is to enforce overarching technical restrictions on infrastructure services. There are simply too many alternatives available, and the technology for the individual access is increasingly easy to use, leading to a constant cat and mouse game between content "owners" and content users.

Taken to its logical conclusion, two extreme scenarios exist. In the first scenario, a few corporations control the online content completely and allow no individual unregulated or unpaid access. In the second scenario, everybody can access all sources on the Internet for free. Both scenarios are unrealistic. Instead, in the foreseeable future it is very likely that we will remain in a state somewhere in-between. The question is, will it be closer to the restricted scenario controlled by a few corporations, or open and – within certain limits – include freely accessible content?

We as content users can influence which of the described scenarios will prevail. The more users access content on the Internet based on the infrastructure as provided, for example, by kimonolabs, Yahoo, IFTTT and others, the more difficult it will become for the "owners" of the content to prevent these solutions, simply because there are too many of them to block technically. This is a practical implementation of the "law of large numbers". And the incentives for users are huge, especially in cases where individual questions with a direct financial impact can be answered based on content derived from the Internet. Just think about the question "Can the Internet inform me the next time United Airlines has a computer glitch in its booking systems?" as an example.

The big Internet companies will have to work tremendously hard if they want to restrict access permanently. It will not be possible to prevent the legal "harvesting" of content on the Internet in the long run. Pursuing a strategy that enables a peaceful coexistence between the providers and users of content on the Internet will be much better for the benefit of all. Reid Hoffman, founder and CEO of LinkedIn, responded to the question what's the benefit for companies if they allow content reuse by third parties: *"happy, connected users"* (McHugh, 2007). Whether this insight will prevail with the major content providers on the Internet in the near future remains doubtful. The central point is the question of how money can be earned with the content. At the end of the day, content providing companies have to finance their services. The conflict will only be solved if a solution can be found that's somehow similar to payment for other shareable goods today. What is needed is a payment model that's fair to and accepted by all sides. Something we have implemented for other shared goods for centuries. Do you use hotels, the energy infrastructure, concerts, movies or theater performances without paying? Certainly not. However, the difference in the digital world is that it is much easier to use content without paying for it. Due to easily accessible digital content, the danger of abuse grows as well. Before we dive into this topic a little deeper, though, let's have a look at a general recipe for how to set up an individual and not-so-easy-to-block tool chain of free services monitoring online stores.

The Monitoring of Online Stores

The following text describes the essential activities to setup the automatic monitoring of online stores. Since every store is structured differently, it could only be a universal explanation, and may require a little tweak here and there to work for your targeted store website. It is highly recommended that you make yourself familiar with kimono, Yahoo Pipes and IFTTT before proceeding with this "recipe". If you have skipped the tutorials for these tools, you should go back and have a look at that material first. If you do not want to create your own online store monitor, you can skip this section and move on to the next chapter.

Please always read and follow the monitored website's terms of use and employ the described tools only when allowed by the website provider. In any case, you must follow every legal requirement for data protection and personal data storage.

Objective:

The continuous monitoring of product or service price developments of an online store.

1) Determine Content Sources

Initially, identifying how the desired content about a product or service (name, price, dealer, delivery time, etc.) can be extracted from the targeted website is required.

If the website provides an RSS or Atom feed for your search or a feed with the latest information on new products, then this is often a good starting point. In these cases, extracting content from the page using a scraper (e.g. kimono) is often not required. If this is the case with your targeted website, move on to step 3).

If the website does not provide a feed containing the required data, the content must be scraped from the page itself. In this case, browse for the desired content and adjust the search results according to your specific informational needs (e.g. sorting by price, scope of results displayed, etc.).

2) Scrape the Content

Start kimono via the bookmarklet in your browser or the Google Chrome plugin and create a new query to scrape the content right from the website. Kimono allows you to select the desired information graphically. The tool automatically tries to select additional content of the same structure. Change this selection until you obtain a satisfactory result. Make sure that you include a unique URL for each entry selected (e.g. a picture link) within your selection. After you have selected the content to be scraped, save the generated selection and choose "CSV" as the output format. Copy the URL of the CSV output generated by kimono to the clipboard.

You can check the data collection created by opening the copied URL in a browser. If everything has worked correctly, your browser will display a comma-separated list of the desired content.

3) Import the Scraped Content into Yahoo Pipes

Open Yahoo Pipes and create a new pipe using the "Create a Pipe" command. If the store website provides a suitable RSS or Atom feed, you can import this feed right into Yahoo Pipes with the module "Fetch Feed". If you have used kimono to set up a CSV output, import the content with the "Fetch CSV" module.

In both cases, you will end up with a data stream in Yahoo Pipes containing all of the content related to the selected products or services for further analysis.

4) Analyze and Manipulate the Results

You can analyze and manipulate the collected content with a variety of Yahoo Pipes functions.

For example, the module "filter" allows you to filter the entire data stream according to a price range for the selected products or services.

5) Export as RSS Feed

Create an individual RSS feed output of your analyzed and manipulated content with the "Create RSS" module. Save the Pipe and return to the dashboard of Yahoo Pipes with the "Back to My Pipes" link. Select the new Pipe in the overview. Yahoo Pipes creates a preview of the generated results. In the upper menu bar of the dashboard, you can choose a variety of output formats for your Pipe. For your first store monitoring exercise, you should start with the "Get as RSS" link and copy it to the clipboard. You can experiment with the other output formats later when you have become more experienced.

6) Automated Querying of the Store Data

Logon to IFTTT and create a new recipe with "Create". Select "Feed" as a triggering channel, and paste the copied URL from Yahoo Pipes into the box asking for the RSS Feed.

IFTTT runs a brief check of the triggering feed to ensure it can be used as a trigger. If IFTTT returns with an error message, the reason is often an unfilled field "RRS Link" in the module "Create RSS" within Yahoo Pipes. In this case, open up

Yahoo Pipes again and add a unique URL by associating the appropriate input data with the module "Create RSS" of Yahoo Pipes. If you obtain the output data from the store directly in the form of an RSS or Atom feed, there is usually a suitable link already present in the input data stream. In this case, just connect the link accordingly. If you have used kimono for extracting the content of a store's web page, you have to use the unique URL included in the selection during step (2).

Select the "Action" that IFTTT should execute when a new product or service – according to the specified filter criteria – is available on the monitored website. For example, you can send yourself an SMS, email, or use services such as Pushover or Boxcar to push messages right to your smartphone.

Note:

The sequence described can of course also be used for other purposes. Any content that can be scraped in a structured way using kimono or that is available as feed can be combined, filtered and analyzed with Yahoo Pipes, whether it is real estate data, equity prices, or gasoline prices, as long as it is legally permissible to do so.

Dirk Stähler

Programmed Abuse

Monitoring for the Masses?

On June 7, 2012, Norddeutscher Rundfunk (NDR), one of the largest public broadcasting companies in Germany, reported on a joint research project of the German credit rating agency SCHUFA and the Potsdam-based Hasso Plattner Institute (HPI). Hasso Plattner, the former CEO and Chairman of the SAP AG software company, founded the HPI, a university excellence center for IT Systems Engineering. The SCHUFA had commissioned the HPI to examine options for the development of consumer profiles based on freely accessible content on the Internet. The joint project was named SCHUFALab@HPI. In addition to data already used by SCHUFA that it had collected at banks, insurance companies, retailers, and various service providers, it was planned to include content derived from open sources on the

Internet in the consumer creditworthiness rating process (Teevs, 2012). The NDR stated in a confidential paper that the SCHUFA and the HPI were planning to collect e-mail addresses, postal addresses, Facebook IDs and other personal characteristics. The plan was to use this personal identification information to search for content created by users on the Internet, and to integrate it into the credit rating process (Hornung & Webermann, 2012). The project sparked considerable resistance from the data protection commissioners of several German states, politicians, and users. The former Federal Commissioner for Data Protection, Peter Schar, commented that he hoped the SCHUFA had informed the responsible data protection authority in the state of Hessen (author's note: legal venue of the SCHUFA) about the project, and would comply with all data protection requirements (Medick & Reißmann, 2012). Comments very quickly flooded the social networks. They ranged from ironic to thoughtful. Hanno Zulla wrote: *"Removed my less wealthy contacts in XING (author's note: German version of LinkedIn), Facebook and Google+. Schufa may come"* (Zulla, 2012). Silke Berz commented more seriously: *"That's what happens when millions of social media experts preach, companies should listen on Twitter and Facebook"* (Berz, 2012). The ideas of the SCHUFA and the HPI frightened the broader public because it was certainly an indication of the possibilities that can arise from evaluating content on the Internet. Experiments of this kind are not limited to companies and research institutions. And with technological progress in mind, it is quite easy to imagine the development in the near future. Every user will be able to create more or less complex evaluations based on the content on the Internet. Today the Internet allows – at least partially – the setup of such solutions. We should not be so naive as to believe that someone somewhere does not already use our personal data. And the development of ever better Internet content evaluations will accelerate. The reason for this is that easy to use tools have arrived on the mass market, and are therefore generally available to everyone:

Collect

There are tools available to easily capture content on the Internet and make it available for further digital processing. Collecting structured digital content from web pages has become a simple task. An example of this type of tool is kimono.

Combine, Filter and Analyze

There are tools available to easily combine, filter and analyze structured digital content. Setting up the automated reaction of a computer system based on a semantic analysis of digital content derived from the Internet has become easy to implement. Even less technically trained users can set up such solutions these days. An example of this type of tool is Yahoo Pipes.

Automate

There are tools available to automate every necessary step for collecting, combining, filtering and analyzing digital content. Even average users without extensive technical knowledge can use them. An example of this type of tool is IFTTT.

Distribute

The infrastructure for mobile access to the Internet is spreading worldwide with double-digit growth rates, ensuring quick and easy access to individually created analyses for every user at any location and any time.

The tools for collecting, combining, filtering and analyzing content on the Internet have been available for some time. But the individual analysis of content collected on the Internet is just beginning to play a significant role in everybody's computing life because the tools have become extremely user-friendly and are available at any time. Simple automation and mobile access make the difference. In other words, we are about to witness the next step in the use of the Internet. Over the coming years, there will be a growing number of individually created solutions based on the content of the Internet. Many of them we cannot even imagine today, ranging from acceptable, to controversial, to illegal solutions based on content scraped from the Internet.

A relevant example of the next step is a platform for data journalism initiated by the British newspaper The Guardian. Readers of the newspaper are invited to evaluate publicly available data from the Internet and provide their results online. A special website was created to distribute and enable access to the results for everybody (http://www.guardian.co.uk/news/datablog). The rationale behind this offer is very simple. The editorial staff in London assumes that the quality of analysis on socially relevant topics increases when experts from the readership are involved. It is expected that this will create more transparency and control of public institutions and companies. The results have proven The Guardian right. Based on reader involvement, the newspaper was able to deliverer interesting news and analytics again and again over the past several years.

Also relevant is the use of content scraped from the Internet for evaluations that provide users with individual value, of course always under the assumption that the underlying content was legally downloaded. Think about the automatic search for information about bargains on products and services as an example. That vendors are less pleased about the fact that "their content" is increasingly used for such evaluations should come as no surprise. From their perspective, this is understandable because the comparison leads to more transparency and competition. Costly vendors will face declining revenues as a consequence. That some of them instead prefer not to take part in this competition is obvious. But the financial benefit of a clever use of the content available on the Internet to every consumer will lead to further dissemination.

In addition to the acceptable use of the content on the Internet, there are also some controversial, and sometimes even legally questionable scenarios. The distinction between the different areas is often blurred. There is, for example, a disagreement as to whether or not the scraping of large quantities of data for commercial use based on third party databases is legally permissible. Even German courts have yet failed to conclusively settle the dispute once and for all. Two independent cases in which travel agencies scraped content from airline websites without permission ended up with different court decisions. The Higher Regional Court of Hamburg considered the "domestic authority" of an airline violated by the fact that their website was used in a form for which it was not intended to be used. Based on this verdict, the airline was entitled to ban the travel agency from their website and prohibit data access (OLG Hamburg, 28.05.2009 - 3 U 191/08).

The Regional Court of Frankfurt came up with a completely contrary judgment, however. In a similar case, the court assumed that the extraction of third party content from a website using screen scraping technology – in other words collecting content directly from a website with tools like kimono – is not a violation of the "domestic authority" of the website's owner (OLG Frankfurt, 05.03.2009 - 6 U 221/08). The preceding discussion on the German Ancillary Copyright Bill reappears in another context besides search engines, again questioning to what extent content may be extracted on third party websites for further use. In June 2011, the German Federal High Court of Justice declared the usage of content from third party databases admissible under certain conditions. If only single specific search queries are made, this activity cannot be considered copying the entire database as a whole because no "essential parts" are affected. If this is the case, then scraping is not a copyright violation (Dittmann, 2011). In the interests of clarity and legal certainty, some additional court decisions are still required.

The dispute makes it clear that it has not yet been decided whether we will experience more freedom or more restrictions when it comes to the individual use of content on the Internet. Much depends on the resolution of legal questions regarding copyrights. But in the long term, content providers will not be able to win this fight legally. The technical capabilities available to the average user are simply evolving too fast. A perfect example is provided by the peer-file-sharing platform Pirate Bay, which was banned by a Swedish court. Since Pirate Bay first went online in 2003, the providers' battle with the authorities responsible for fighting Internet piracy within different countries has continued, resulting in a perfect cat-and-mouse game. Today, the source code of the software is freely available, enabling practically anyone to create a clone of the platform on the Internet. And a few developers have already made use of it. If a server outside of Germany, where local courts have no influence, provides the platform, the legal sword of German authorities quickly becomes blunt. Only a massive intervention in the technical infrastructure of the Internet can result in sustained success for the opponents of free content access. But in this case, everyone would suffer from reduced innovation speed, limited information opportunities and plurality, and a general threat to freedom of speech. Ernesto Van Der Sar (pseudonym), founder of the copyright and piracy site Torrent-Freak, recommended that content providers should finally quit the fight against piracy. Attempts to seek legal solutions have been running for years with no apparent success. Instead, companies should begin to experiment with new forms of content distribution (Bilton, 2012).

But even if the dispute over the German Ancillary Copyright Bill is eventually settled, one critical issue remains: the collection and analysis of personal data, especially when it is done without the knowledge and influence of those affected. The ideas of the SCHUFA credit rating agency and the Hasso-Plattner-Institut were not the first attempt to extract marketable information from the content on the Internet. In May 2010, it was revealed that the market research company Nielsen monitored a forum for patients with mental illness. This was done on behalf of a client within the pharmaceutical industry. By analyzing published forum entries, Nielsen and its client wanted to gain insights into the use and reviews of certain pharmaceutical products by the patients. As a "by-product", personal data that could be used to identify individual participants in the forum was collected as well (Angwin & Stecklow, 2010).

There is already an intense commercial data analysis business out there based on our individual data that is freely available on the Internet that most of us are not aware of due to a lack of public interest. Or did you know that the German infas geodaten GmbH analyzes up to 19.6 million buildings in Germany for *"socio-demographics, health data, consumer and leisure behavior, car ownership and residential environment and location information"* (Infas Geodaten, 2013)? This might not surprise a reader in the U.S., but taken into consideration in a country like Germany with its strong data protection laws, that nobody really cares is a little bit frightening. We have already gotten used to the practice that our individual data is commercially processed and used. Yet are we no longer concerned when our data privacy is at risk?

Most people are probably not aware that there are databases on the Internet searching for all Facebook user IDs, including first name, last name, gender and location. The only thing required to access this information is to know its URL.

In the future, comprehensive data analyses based on Internet content will be available for everyone. It will be possible to collect, analyze, modify and distribute content with little effort. Integrating somebody else's private and personal data within complex analyses will only require a few clicks in a browser. And a specific risk will emerge from the increasingly straightforward way of automating all of the necessary steps. Even an average user will no longer be forced to sit down in front of his computer and manually browse all of the required data. All necessary steps for comprehensive data analysis on the Internet will be available at the click of a button. The idea of the SCHUFA credit rating agency and the Hasso Plattner Institute is no longer so far away. The only difference is that the capability will not be limited to governmental agencies or large corporations. Almost everybody will be able to do this. These capabilities are neither good nor bad. It depends on the way we are going to use them that makes the difference. Irrespective of this fact, one thing is clear: only if we understand these tools will we be able to make a lawful use of them for personal benefit and protect ourselves from misuse.

The Monitoring of Internet Forums

The following text describes the essential steps to the setup of an automatic monitoring of Internet forums. Since every Internet forum is structured differently, it could only be a universal explanation and may require a little tweak here and there to make it work on your targeted forum. It is highly recommended that you make yourself familiar with kimono, Yahoo Pipes and IFTTT before proceeding with this "recipe". If you have skipped the tutorials for these tools, you should go back and have a look at that material first. If you do not want to create your own forum monitor, you can skip this section and move on to the next chapter.

The initial steps of this "recipe" are identical to the previously described monitoring of online stores. To assure a complete description of the procedures required to set up a monitoring solution, I have repeated them. A new aspect of forum monitoring is the automatic collection of content within cloud storage, a computing model in which data is stored on remote servers accessible from the Internet.

Please as always read and follow the monitored website's terms of use, and employ the described tools only when allowed by the website provider. In any case, you must follow every legal requirement for data protection and the storage of personal data.

Objective: The continuous monitoring of posts on Internet forums and automatic keyword-based storage of selected posts in cloud storage for later analysis.

1) Determine Content Sources

Initially, identifying how the desired posts can be extracted from the targeted website is required. If the website provides an RSS or Atom feed for new posts, this is often a good starting point, and using a scraper (e.g. kimono) is often not required. If this is the case with your targeted website, move on to step 3).

If the website does not provide a feed containing the required data, the content must be scraped from the page itself. In this case, browse for the desired content and adjust the search results according to your specific informational needs (e.g. category of posts, etc.).

2) Scrape the Content

Start kimono via the bookmarklet in your browser or the Google Chrome plugin, and create a new query to scrape the content right from the targeted website. Kimono allows you to select the desired information graphically. The tool automatically tries to select additional content of the same structure. Change this selection until you obtain a satisfactory result. Make sure that you include a unique URL for each entry selected (e.g. a link of each post) within your selection. After you have selected the content to be scraped, save the generated selection and choose "CSV" as the output format. Copy the URL of the CSV output generated by kimono to the clipboard.

You can check the data collection created by opening the copied URL in a browser. If everything works correctly, your browser will display a comma-separated list of the desired content.

3) Import the Scraped Content into Yahoo Pipes

Open Yahoo Pipes and create a new pipe using the "Create a Pipe" command. If the forum provides a suitable RSS or Atom feed, you can import this feed right into Yahoo Pipes with the module "Fetch Feed". If you have used kimono to set up a CSV output, import the content with the "Fetch CSV" module.

In both cases you will end up with a data stream in Yahoo Pipes containing the content of all selected forum posts for further analysis.

4) Analyze and Manipulate the Results

You can analyze and manipulate the collected content with a variety of Yahoo Pipes functions. For example, the module "filter" allows you to filter the entire data stream according to keywords within the posts. If you are looking for posts on a specific topic, Yahoo Pipes will only forward content that matches the defined keywords.

5) Export as RSS Feed

Create an individual RSS feed output of your analyzed and manipulated content with the "Create RSS" module. Save the Pipe and return to the dashboard of Yahoo Pipes with the "Back to My Pipes" link. Select the new Pipe in the overview.

Yahoo Pipes creates a preview of the generated results. In the upper menu bar of the dashboard, you can choose a variety of output formats for your Pipe. For your first forum monitoring exercise, you should start with the "Get as RSS" link and copy it to the clipboard. You can experiment with the other output formats later when you have become more experienced.

6) Automated Forum Querying

Logon to IFTTT and create a new recipe with "Create". Select "Feed" as the triggering channel and paste the copied URL from Yahoo Pipes into the box asking for the RSS Feed.

IFTTT runs a brief check of the triggering feed to ensure it can be used as a trigger. If IFTTT returns with an error message, the reason often is an unfilled "RRS Link" field in the module "Create RSS" within Yahoo Pipes. In this case, open up Yahoo Pipes again and add a unique URL at the "Link" attribute in the module "Create RSS" of Yahoo Pipes. If you obtain the output data from the forum directly in the form of an RSS or Atom feed, there is usually a suitable URL already present in the input data stream. In this case, just connect the link accordingly. If you have used kimono for extracting the content of a forum's web page, you have to use the unique URL included in this selection during step (2).

Select the "Action" that IFTTT should execute when a new post – according to the specified filter criteria – appears on the monitored forum. If you want to save all of the collected posts within the Internet, you could use a cloud storage service. IFTTT offers connections for Dropbox, OneDrive or Google Drive. For example, you could set up an IFTTT recipe that automatically adds a new row to a Google spreadsheet whenever a new post appears in the forum. All of the required work is carried out automatically by web-based services. You don't have to keep your computer online. All of the content collected can be retrieved from the cloud storage whenever you like.

Note:

The sequence described can of course be used for other purposes. Any content that can be scraped in a structured way using kimono, or that is available as a feed, can be combined, filtered and analyzed with Yahoo Pipes as long as it is legally permissible to do so.

The Do-It-Yourself NSA?

In May 2013, Eric Schmidt, Executive Chairman of Google, expressed his thoughts about the increase of surveillance at the British newspaper The Telegraph: *"You have to fight for your privacy, or you will lose it"* (Colvile, 2013). The safest approach to fighting for privacy is not to publish personal data at all. But we have to admit that in the Web 3.0 age, this approach is no longer realistic. We cannot avoid producing personal information on the web whenever we are online. Therefore, it is increasingly important to recognize the threats and risks we face on the Internet today in addition to the many opportunities that have been opened up by the availability of a worldwide network accessible to everyone.

One example in particular shows how carelessly many on the Internet express personal content: Facebook postings. The social network Facebook is well known all over the world. Since its founding in 2004, the company has continually expanded. In 2012, more than 1 billion users were actively posting on Facebook. By then, worldwide users had produced more than 300 million photos and 3.2 billion comments and Likes (an expression users can employ to express approval of given entries on Facebook) every day (Website-Monitoring.com, 2012). At the end of 2012, around 25 million users were registered on the social network in Germany, or 2.5 percent of the world's registered Facebook users. Recalculated in relation to the total number of photos, comments and Likes, this resulted in 7.5 million photos and 80 million comments and Likes that were created daily. This content contains very personal information, much of it public. Anyone can search for these entries on Facebook as long as the user hasn't turned on increased security settings for their Facebook profile. Unfortunately – or fortunately for the data scrapers – many users do not make use of these settings. And the techniques for searching the constant stream of Facebook postings are easy to apply and well-described by Facebook on its own help pages.

Facebook provides access for targeted searches based on keywords and specific terms. The easiest way to do this is by entering a search query right within your browser's URL field called Facebook Graph API. The corresponding Internet address is https://graph.facebook.com. If you type this URL into a web browser, you'll initially receive an error message; it requires additional parameters to selectively output data. With a simple supplement, for example, personal identification data can be queried for each registered user. You only have to extend the URL by the user's Facebook name:

https://graph.facebook.com/<Facebook Name>

The result is a machine-readable list of the user's first and last name, gender, language setting and the unique Facebook ID. Although the output includes a unique Facebook ID, the result provides no further information, but with a simple extension of the URL and the unique Facebook ID, you could start building a Facebook monitor.

Let's have a look at the URL extension first. Use the following URL to search for a specific term, written in single quotation marks, within Facebook's data stream:

https://graph.facebook.com/search?q=<'Search Term'>&type=post&access_token=<Access Token>

To make this query work, an access code – called an Access Token – is required. This access code identifies the request sent to the Facebook search interface. Once received, access to the requested data is granted. Facebook provides this access code for any registered user through a free additional registration as a Facebook developer. You can easily do this within your own Facebook profile. Within a few seconds, the required code appears within your Facebook account and the door to query Facebook's data stream is wide open.

The only problem that remains is the limited ability of the Facebook Graph API to combine or exclude different search terms within a single search. Logical queries to link different search terms often cannot be realized. At this point, Yahoo Pipes comes into play. Yahoo Pipes allows you to set up multiple Facebook search queries in parallel, and to filter and sort the collected data by individual criteria. With Yahoo Pipes, it is easy to create an individual Facebook data stream and use it for further processing on the Internet as an RSS feed. Finally, the only thing required to set up a 24/7 running Facebook monitor without any personal infrastructure requirements at zero cost is to ensure that the data stream is continuously stored. This is where IFTTT comes in handy. In combination with cloud storage services such as Dropbox or Google Drive, IFTTT ensures that interesting Facebook posts are automatically recorded and stored for later evaluation.

It can be shown that a nearly consistent observation of the public Facebook posting stream for an individual user can be achieved with the setup of just three independent Yahoo Pipes and IFTTT monitoring combinations. Just to make it clear once again: this requires nothing more than an Internet connection. No software, no infrastructure, and almost no specific technical knowledge. In order to describe it a little ironically, some government agencies spend much more for such capability.

The combination of web-based services described could be used the other way around as well. Every post collected includes the Facebook ID, and it is easy to identify Facebook users by this individual identification number. Based on the personal information of a Facebook page, often publicly available, further conclusions are possible. Compromising posts such as complaints about jobs, private relationships or offensive remarks against other users can quickly have consequences, consequences that in most of the cases are certainly not desired by their authors.

Some examples of public status messages from Facebook users that might cost them their jobs, or could at least create some difficulties if they became public in their personal environment, include:

"I can transform a rising 'Kiss my a.., man' into a clear 'Yes boss'"

"My boss asked me today to show the trainee what I am doing here all day... since this morning he is also on Facebook"

"I get up every morning at 5:30 commute to my [expletive] job one and a half hours where my [expletive] of a boss expects me to kiss his [expletive] all day"

"We have a new boss. As an [expletive] still glossed over. Will quickly leave for another company"

The Higher Labor Court in Hamm, Germany declared in a decision on October 10, 2012 that the instant termination of an employment agreement is admissible based on negative statements made on Facebook. Offenses that pose significant libel in form and content are a violation of employee obligations under an existing employment relationship (Golem.de, 2012).

Based on publicly available Facebook profiles, conclusions regarding the identification of a specific individual can be drawn. And even if not every status message on Facebook has legal implications, do you want your boss, your neighbors or family members automatically snooping around in your private postings? Or the neighborhood thief?

More generally, would it be possible to monitor and analyze the daily flood of data consisting of 7.5 million photos and 80 million comments and Likes, or can we still rely on the principle of "Anonymity through obscurity"?

Loosely translated, "Anonymity through obscurity" expresses the situation that the amount of data alone guarantees certain anonymity, although the content itself is not protected. It is obvious that this approach does not offer protection from professional and governmental data collectors, a fact known already before Edward Snowden revealed the interception of Internet traffic by the NSA and other intelligence services. The question is, can this approach be considered safe for monitoring attempts carried out by the average Internet user without comprehensive technology expertise and technical resources? Is it guaranteed that your neighbor, employer, or any other person with an interest, whether it is legitimate or not, cannot to a larger extent start to sniff around in your personal Facebook data? In consideration of the available Internet services for the collection, combination, analysis and automated distribution of content, this is no longer ensured. The barrier is full of holes. Reliable protection against prying eyes is definitely no longer guaranteed.

It should be noted that in this context, the German Data Protection Act prohibits the collection of personal data unless the data owner gives prior written approval. But the technical capabilities for monitoring will continue to improve, regardless of whether the use is legal or not in any particular case. The tools for the collection, combination, filtering, analysis, automation, and distribution of content on the Internet will progress. This will allow more and more people to access the content available on the World Wide Web. Even if legal obstacles try to prevent this abuse, its development will continue. Take the German Data Protection Act as example. Germany has one of the strongest data protection laws in the world, but if there is a technology allowing every single citizen to collect personal data and store it privately somewhere on the Internet, who will be able to prosecute this? What is the value in having a strong data protection law in effect that nobody can enforce?

We as users have to deal with the fact that it is impossible to completely control all conceivable scenarios for the collection of personal data on the Internet. In particular, the easier it is to access content on the Internet, the more frequently it will be done. To be protected, at least a little bit, the mechanisms of the simplest attacks on personal data must be clearly understood by everyone. Those who can defend themselves from these forms of attacks will be slightly more secure.

The safest solution would be to publish no more personal posts on the Internet. Eric Schmidt commented on this approach a bit further speculating: *"If you have something that you don't want anyone to know, maybe you shouldn't be doing it in the first place"* (Bartiromo, 2009).

As a society, we have to avoid building up paranoia just because we are afraid that our friends, neighbors, colleagues and others who have an interest - justified or not – could spy on us with simple and generally accessible technical solutions. It is important that we are always aware of how vulnerable we make ourselves through the unreflective dissemination of personal information on the Internet. So for me, Eric Schmidt's view is confirmed on at least one point: private information is no longer private in any case. And it is highly likely that this will stay that way.

Monitoring Your Digital Shadow

The following text describes the essential activities to set up automatic monitoring of your personal Internet shadow. Specifically, that means the information that is published about you on the World Wide Web. Since different sources for collecting the required data are available, this can only be a universal explanation, and may require a little tweak here and there to adopt it to your individual needs. It is highly recommended that you make yourself familiar with IFTTT before proceeding with this "recipe". If you have skipped the tutorials for this tool, you should go back and have a look at that material first. If you do not want to create your own digital shadow monitor, you can skip this section and move on to the next chapter.

Please always read and follow the terms of use for any website used, and employ the described tools only when allowed by the website provider.

In any case, you must follow every legal requirement for data protection and personal data storage.

Objective: The continuous monitoring of posts on the Internet relating to oneself and the storing of entries found in cloud storage for later analysis.

1) Determine Content Sources

The monitoring of posts published on the Internet about oneself initially appears very complicated. Actually, it would require the regular scanning of the entire Internet – or at least as much as possible – for content related to you.

Fortunately, there are tools available that take care of a substantial part of this monitoring: search engines. To keep an eye on the content related to oneself, you only have to use one of the major search engines as a content "scanner".

The starting point is a search about oneself that is designed as precisely as possible. This means creating a search query that matches criteria describing you as extensively as possible. Make use of the advanced search options to target specific word combinations with quotation marks, or exclude terms from the query when they produce results that do not belong to you. The key is to customize the search describing you as closely as possible. You should experiment a little with different keywords until you're satisfied with the result, but don't overdue it. You have to deal with a certain amount of imprecision.

If you use Bing as a search engine, move on to step 2. If you use Google as a search engine, go to step 3.

2) Preparing Bing Results

With a simple extension of the URL, Bing provides the search results as an RSS feed. The only thing required is to supplement it with the following expression:

&format=rss&count=50

The "count" parameter at the end specifies the maximum number of hits returned. Currently Bing allows 50 RSS entries for each search executed. This is good for about four to five search result pages and should be sufficient for the most people searching for a name. The result is available directly as an RSS feed. After you have created and tested the search URL, move on to step 4.

3) Preparing Google Results

Google can be used for monitoring as well, although there is no RSS output available. To set up Google, you have to use the "Alerts" function. All that is required is a Google account and an e-mail address at Google's mail service, Gmail, especially intended for receiving your search results. Set up a Google Alert for your individual search that will send an email for each new search result found on the Internet directly to this Gmail address. After you have set up this alarm, move on to step 5.

4) Automatically Query the Content for Bing

Logon to IFTTT and create a new recipe with "Create". Select "Feed" as a triggering channel, and paste the created Bing search URL into the box asking for the RSS feed. Select the "Action" that IFTTT should execute when a new entry appears within the search. For example, you can send yourself an SMS, email, or use services such as Pushover or Boxcar to push information right to your smartphone.

5) Automatically Query the Content for Google

Logon to IFTTT and create a new recipe with "Create". Select "Gmail" as a triggering channel and "Any new mail" as the specific trigger. Select the "Action" that IFTTT should execute when a new entry appears within the search. For example, you can send yourself an SMS, email, or use services such as Pushover or Boxcar to push information right to your smartphone.

Note:

The described sequence can, of course, also be used for other monitoring purposes. All searchable content on the Internet can be monitored this way. This includes news about a company, products and services, and much more. Please always read and follow the terms of use of any website and tool used.

Dirk Stähler

Epilogue

Somebody Asleep?

The Internet has come a long way since its invention in the 1960s. Initially based on a relatively small group of computers of scientists and American universities, it has evolved from a communication medium for computer geeks into a global information platform. The ideas of Timothy Berners-Lee have made it possible for more people worldwide to have access to a medium for the exchange of information of all kinds, and the numbers are increasing daily.

Whether you look at the number of users, the sum of connected devices, the number of available websites, the amount of data generated and stored, or the amount of content exchanged, in all respects, the Internet has shown impressive growth over the last twenty years, and has reached new dimensions every year. As new records are set, the significance of the role content plays on the Internet will only increase. These records would have never been possible without the specific value derived from the content on the Internet for every single user. Anyone who is capable of utilizing the content of the Internet has an advantage over others who can't. Last, but not least financially, experienced users gain a financial benefit of up to $2,000 per year compared with those who don't when utilizing the content of the Internet in order to become better informed and make better decisions.

But it has been a long journey to get to where we are today, starting with the Web 1.0 - Web of Documents - progressing to the Web 2.0 - Web of Content – and moving forward to the Web 3.0 - Web of Data – which lies ahead of us. During this journey, we have observed serious upheavals on the Internet every ten years. With the Web 3.0, we are currently experiencing the next change. Many might still see this as a development toward a standardized Web 3.0 where generally binding rules for the automated processing of content on the Internet will be established. This will not occur. The standardized semantic web as defined by the W3C is dead. It is much more likely that we will evolve toward an individual semantic web where each user, according to its own criteria, mixes content. Some of the required tools to make this scenario a reality have existed for some time, some new tools are currently out there, and many more will be in development while you read this book. Common to all of them is that they are – and will be even more – available and usable by everyone. In the coming years, they will continue to improve, become even easier to use, and gain more and more importance for the utilization of the content on the Internet. The reason for this development is that the capabilities to collect, combine, filter, analyze, automate and access content on the Internet will enable individual usage scenarios that did not previously exist. In the future, whenever the "standard" Internet does not provide appropriate solutions for the individual information requirements of its users, we will create our own services. And there will be even more individual solutions created, the simpler the development becomes. Already today, extensive technical knowledge is no longer required. Technical progress will continue to drive this development. Individually utilized content is about to change our use of the Internet. The techniques and tools for collection, processing and automated response of the Internet presented in this book are only at the very early stages of the changes towards an Internet that "thinks".

More and more devices will be given direct access to the Internet. The real world and its processes are increasingly digitized. The Internet of Things – a computing concept where everyday physical objects will be connected to the Internet and be able to exchange data with each other – will produce even more content that can potentially be processed. Automobiles, consumer products, home automation, medical equipment, clothing, and many more devices will produce content for and about us in the near future. Whether we like it or not, the trend is unstoppable.

Sometime between January 1, 2008 and December 31, 2009, for the first time, more devices were connected to the Internet than human beings living on the planet. In 2010, the number of Internet-enabled devices was estimated to be 12.5 billion. For 2015, experts expect 20 billion, and in 2020, 50 billion devices are predicted to be communicating over the Internet (Evans, 2011). Individual solutions for accessing and processing content, easy to set up and maintain by everybody, will be absolutely necessary to supplement conventional approaches to the utilization of the knowledge on the Internet. A public solution will not be created for every conceivable information requirement. Therefore, it is crucial that every Internet user be capable of accessing and processing the content on the Internet individually. The automation of our lives on the basis of content of the World Wide Web will acquire a significance that is not fully conceivable today. And the company that is about to provide us with the required infrastructure will be the next Google.

Two types of companies have a good probability of regaining lost ground in existing markets: the media industry and network infrastructure providers. It is incomprehensible that publishers, media and telecommunication companies do not actively take advantage of this opportunity. Instead of opening up the market and continuing to develop it, they call for legal hurdles, such as the Ancillary Copyright Bill in Germany, or the restrictions on net neutrality (author's note: net neutrality requires Internet service providers to treat all data on the Internet equally). Both types of corporations already possess the essential skills to make this happen.

For publishers and media companies, the opportunity is to develop a business model that is based on their original core competency: creating and providing edited valuable content. For the first time in many years, they would be able to generate significant revenues that are not based on advertising alone. If they could further develop their position as "navigators in a jungle of content", providing tools and services for an extended individual processing of content as well, this would offer real value for their customers. The advantage to publishing and media companies is that they are familiar with the work of editorial preparation of content, a skill that will become more and more important as the amount of data available on the Internet increases. This is still their core business - or should be, at least. They should have a sense for pre-processing valuable content on the Internet, making it available for further individual use.

Telecommunications companies could critically shape the emerging market as well. As providers of network infrastructure, their services are almost interchangeable today. If they would start to offer their own solutions for an individual use of the content on the Internet, this could reduce the willingness of their customers to switch to another provider. This would address one of the core problems they face today: the competition for flat rates and bandwidth, a contest no supplier can win in the long run. Furthermore, they could bundle these individual services with the devices they offer to their customers, improving their position against the dominant manufacturers of smartphones and tablets. Following such an approach, telecommunications providers would have the opportunity to develop the "operating system" of the individual Web 3.0 on top of their network, a strengthening of their market position that should not be underestimated. The advantage to the large network infrastructure providers is that most of them already have the resources required to develop the solutions needed. Most of them own IT service companies that possess the experience and knowledge to implement the services.

Where is the Market and Who Pays for the Services?

One thing is certain: companies that manage to establish services for the collection, processing, analysis and distribution of content on the Internet have a realistic chance of above average growth rates. Take IFTTT as example. In the second half of 2011, the company observed an increase in individual solutions created using their system by more than 500 percent (IFTTT, 2011). The model of becoming an infrastructure provider for the collection, processing, analysis and distribution of content is attractive from a cost and revenue perspective. It allows these companies to restrict themselves to the development of core services, such as web scraping or Internet automation. The development, operation and maintenance cost of such "generic" services is significantly lower compared with the cost of providing specific individual content-based solutions for the virtually unlimited information needs of Internet users.

And potential customers – everyone who wants to gain more value from the content on the Internet – will not run out of ideas any time soon. When there is real value provided by these services, we will be willing to pay for them. Just the automatic delivery of travel coupons via a combination of Yahoo Pipes and IFTTT services saved me more than $500 in hotel fees in 2013. A few dollars of usage fees for the service would definitely be worth the money I am willing to pay for them. Of course I like using the services without having to pay for them, but I certainly would be willing to pay. The venture capital currently invested in companies like IFTTT and kimonolabs confirms that at least a few investors recognize this opportunity.

There is nothing wrong with thinking about completely new business models based on the cooperation of infrastructure providers and power users in the near future. Whoever develops clever solutions based on generic services could market them together with the infrastructure providers. Maybe this will create a whole new ecosystem of individual solutions to manage our digital daily life, similar to the introduction of App-Stores a few years ago. At that time, a market was created through the combination of smartphones and tablets with a new class of software that did not exist before. Why shouldn't something similar succeed a second time with "individual content based solutions"? If someone comes up with a clever solution that is capable of sending me an alert whenever the booking system of a major airline "goes crazy" – to be more precise, a solution that works better than my own – why shouldn't I pay a few bucks for the idea?

There is a whole world of ideas out there building upon content derived from the Internet. As Michael Saylor describes in his book "The Mobile Wave", new technologies do not necessarily replace existing ones. Rather, they produce not previously anticipated new solutions (Saylor, 2012). If the individual use of the content of the Internet is available for everyone, we will witness these types of new solutions.

But there are risks. The old and new tools – a few of them have been described within this book – to gain individual value out of the content on the Internet can also turn against us. It's like that with many things in life. The way in which those tools are utilized determines whether a given use is sensible, or even questionable. As a digital society, we still have no common understanding of what a meaningful use might look like and where boundaries required to be accepted by everyone would have to be drawn. It will take some time before the rules can be defined.

But until then, time will not stand still. The tools and services explained within this book can be used to make the Internet work for us. We can create financial market monitors to help us improve our investment decisions. We can observe the change in prices for products and services in order to secure a bargain. We can collect content on the Internet to provide raw data that helps answer questions based on further analysis. We can automate recurring tasks in our digital daily life, and much more.

It is not yet clear who will ultimately develop and market these new solutions. But one thing is certain: providers and consumers of content will have to agree on a new business model that ensures a reasonable compensation for the content derived from the Internet. Take me as example. As an author, I have an interest in ensuring that my work is not distributed free of charge because I invested a lot of time and effort in it. The work on this book alone has taken some time. If you have read and received it for free - from wherever - I ask you to subsequently purchase it. Perhaps this is the first compromise in the new world of utilizing digital content: flipping the process of paying and using. This requires trust on the side of producers, and honesty on the part of users.

Bibliography

Accenture. (2011). Mobile Web Watch 2011 (p. 44). Retrieved from http://www.accenture.com/SiteCollectionDocuments/Local_Germany/PDF/Accenture-Studie-Mobile-Web-Watch-2011.pdf

Accenture. (2012). The 2012 Accenture Consumer Electronics Products and Services Usage Report (p. 21). Retrieved from http://www.accenture.com/SiteCollectionDocuments/PDF/Accenture_EHT_Research_2012_Consumer_Technology_Report.pdf

ACSI. (2012). Facebook Plummets; Google+ Strong in American Customer Satisfaction Index. American Customer Satisfaction Index. Retrieved on August 9, 2013 from http://www.theacsi.org/media-resources/press-release-july-2012

Anderson, C. (2006). The Long Tail: How Endless Choice Is Creating Unlimited Demand. (A. Chris, Ed.) Word Journal Of The International Linguistic Association (p. 256). Random House Business Books. Retrieved from http://www.amazon.co.uk/dp/184413850X

Angwin, J., & Stecklow, S. (2010). "Scrapers" Dig Deep for Data on Web. The Wall Street Journal. Retrieved on January 3, 2013 from http://online.wsj.com/article/SB10001424052748 703358504575544381288117888.html#

Apple Inc. (2010). Apple Announces iPad. Retrieved from https://itunes.apple.com/de/podcast/apple-keynotes/id275834665#

Bartiromo, M. (2009). Google's Privacy. Retrieved from http://video.cnbc.com/gallery/?play=1&video= 1372176413

Battelle, J. (2005). The Search: How Google and Its Rivals Rewrote the Rules of Business and Transformed Our Culture. Portfolio The Magazine Of The Fine Arts (pp. 1–329). Portfolio.

Baye, M. R., Morgan, J., & Scholten, P. (2003). The Value of Information in an Online Consumer Electronics Market. Journal of Public Policy Marketing, 22(1), 17–25. doi:10.1509/jppm.22.1.17.17625

Berners-Lee, T., Hendler, J., & Lassila, O. (2001). The Semantic Web. Scientific American, 284(5), 34–43. doi:10.1038/scientificamerican0501-34

Berz, S. (2012). Das kommt davon, wenn Millionen von Social Media Experten predigen, Unternehmen sollten bei Twitter und Facebook zuhören. Twitter. Retrieved from https://twitter.com/paulinepauline/status/210649978975166464

Bilton, N. (2012). Internet Pirates Will Always Win. The New York Times. Retrieved on January 23, 2013 from https://www.nytimes.com/2012/08/05/sunday-review/internet-pirates-will-always-win.html

BuiltWith.com. (2013). RSS Usage Statistics. Retrieved on February 17, 2013 from http://trends.builtwith.com/feeds/RSS

Cachelin, J. L. (2012). HRM Trend Studie 2012 (p. 42). St. Gallen. Retrieved from http://www.wissensfabrik.ch/downloads/Erzeugnisse_Studien/hrm_studie_150dpi_Screen.pdf

Carlson, C. N. (2003). Information Overload , Retrieval Strategies and Internet User Empowerment. In L. Haddon (Ed.), The Good, the Bad and the Irrelevant (COST 269) (pp. 169–173). Helsinki (Finland): Media Lab UIAH. Retrieved from http://hdl.handle.net/10760/5432

Carna. (2013). Internet Census 2012. Retrieved on March 22, 2013 from http://internetcensus2012.bitbucket.org/paper.html

Cisco. (2013). Cisco Visual Networking Index. Retrieved on July 24, 2013 from http://www.cisco.com/en/US/solutions/collateral/ns341/ns525/ns537/ns705/ns827/white_paper_c11-481360.pdf

Colvile, R. (2013). Eric Schmidt interview: "You have to fight for your privacy or you will lose it." The Telegraph. Retrieved on October 7, 2013 from http://www.telegraph.co.uk/technology/eric-schmidt/10076175/Eric-Schmidt-interview-You-have-to-fight-for-your-privacy-or-you-will-lose-it.html

ComScore. (2012). 2012 Mobile Future in Focus.

DiNucci, D. (1999). Fragmented Future. Print, 53(4), 32ff. Retrieved from http://darcyd.com/fragmented_future.pdf

Dittmann, M. (2011). Bundesgerichtshof zum Screen Scraping: Auslesen von Datenbanken durch Bots. Retrieved on August 19, 2013 from http://www.onlinelaw.de/de/aktuelles/it_news .php?we_objectID=300&pid=0

Downes, S. (2007). Why the Semantic Web Will Fail. Half an Hour. Retrieved on November 15, 2012 from http://halfanhour.blogspot.de/2007/03/why-semantic-web-will-fail.html

Evans, D. (2011). The Internet of Things - How the Next Evolution of the Internet Is Changing Everything (p. 11). Retrieved from http://www.cisco.com/web/about/ac79/docs/i nnov/IoT_IBSG_0411FINAL.pdf

Facebook. (2013). Statement of Rights and Responsibilities. Retrieved on July 19, 2014 from https://www.facebook.com/legal/terms

Forrest, C. (2014). How Kimono Labs can turn any website into an API. TechRepublic. Retrieved on July 5, 2014 from http://www.techrepublic.com/article/how-kimono-labs-can-turn-any-website-into-an-api/

Frucci, A. (2010). 8 Things That Suck About the iPad. Gizmodo. Retrieved on May 31, 2013 from http://gizmodo.com/5458382/8-things-that-suck-about-the-ipad

Gansky, L. (2010). The Mesh: Why the Future of Business Is Sharing (p. 256). Portfolio Hardcover.

Gantz, J. F., & Reinsel, D. (2011). Extracting Value from Chaos. IDC iView, (June), 1–12. Retrieved from http://idcdocserv.com/1142

Gantz, J. F., Reinsel, D., Chute, C., Schlichting, W., McArthur, J., Minton, S., … Manfrediz, A. (2007). The Expanding Digital Universe.

Golem.de. (2012). Entlassung wegen Facebook-Äußerungen ist rechtens. Golem.de. Retrieved on November 2, 2013 from http://www.golem.de/news/landesarbeitsgeric ht-hamm-entlassung-wegen-facebook-aeusserungen-ist-rechtens-1301-96930.html

Google. (2012). Unser mobiler Planet: Deutsch-land Der mobile Nutzer. Retrieved from http://services.google.com/fh/files/blogs/our_mobile_planet_germany_de.pdf

Google. (2014a). Google Terms of Service. Re-trieved on July 19, 2014 from http://www.google.com/intl/us/policies/terms/regional.html

Google. (2014b). Privacy Policy. Retrieved on July 19, 2014 from http://www.google.com/intl/us/policies/privacy/

Gray, I. A. (2013). Welcome to Twools– RSS Feeds for Twitter and more! iag.me. Retrieved on August 16, 2013 from http://iag.me/twools/

Hammell, R., Perricos, C., Branch, D., & Lewis, H. (2011). Unlocking growth How open data creates new opportunities for the UK (p. 42). Retrieved from http://www.deloitte.com/assets/Dcom-UnitedKingdom/Local As-sets/Documents/Market insights/Deloitte Ana-lytics/uk-mi-da-unlocking-growth.pdf

Hay, D. (2010). Web 3 . 0 demystified : An expla-nation in pictures. Technorati. Retrieved on Oc-tober 9, 2012 from http://technorati.com/technology/article/web-30-demystified-an-explanation-in/

Heidemann, J., Pradkin, Y., Govindan, R., Papa-dopoulos, C., Bartlett, G., & Bannister, J. (2008). Census and survey of the visible internet. Pro-ceedings of the 8th ACM SIGCOMM Conference on Internet Measurement Conference IMC 08, 169. doi:10.1145/1452520.1452542

Hornung, P., & Webermann, J. (2012). Was hat die Schufa mit Facebook vor? NDR Info. Re-trieved on February 27, 2013 from http://www.ndr.de/ratgeber/netzwelt/schufa1 21.html

IAB Europe. (2010). Consumers driving the digital uptake. Europe (p. 27). Retrieved from http://iabeurope.eu/media/39559/whitepaper _consumerdrivingdigitaluptake_final.pdf

IDC. (2013). Tablet Shipments Soar to Record Levels During Strong Holiday Quarter. Retrieved from http://www.idc.com/getdoc.jsp?containerId=pr US23926713#.UQqxL79EF16

IFTTT. (2011). ifttt one year in. IFTTT Blog. Retrieved on October 31, 2013 from http://blog.ifttt.com/post/14219635005/ifttt-one-year-in

IFTTT. (2012). Upcoming changes to Twitter Triggers. Retrieved on June 21, 2013 from http://updates.ifttt.com/post/31945038639/upc oming-changes-to-twitter-triggers

Indvik, L. (2012). Publishers Begin Pulling Advertising From Flipboard. www.Mashable.com. Retrieved on December 27, 2012 from http://mashable.com/2012/06/25/flipboard-new-yorker-wired-advertising/

Infas Geodaten. (2013). Mikrogeographische Daten. Retrieved on June 24, 2013 from http://www.infas-geodaten.de/index.php?id=52

Internet World Stats. (2012). Internet Growth Statistics. Retrieved on October 15, 2012 from http://www.internetworldstats.com/emarketing .htm

Interrogare. (2012). Digitale Mediennutzung im Zeitalter von Tablets, Smartphones und Apps (p. 8). Retrieved from http://www.interrogare.de/news/news-detailansicht/trendstudie-2012-smartphones-und-tablets-dominieren-die-private-mediennutzung-apps-bevorzugt/da3452c23f29844a70a7897ffb5feb0c/

Kirkpatrick, M. (2010). How Yahoo's Latest Acquisition Stole & Broke My Heart. www.readwrite.com. Retrieved on December 7, 2012 from http://readwrite.com/2010/10/15/when

Klessmann, J., Denker, P., Schieferdecker, I., & Schulz, S. E. (2012). Open Government Data Deutschland (p. 572).

Kobie, N. (2010). Q&A: Conrad Wolfram on communicating with apps in Web 3.0. IT PRO. Retrieved on October 25, 2012 from http://www.itpro.co.uk/621535/q-a-conrad-wolfram-on-communicating-with-apps-in-web-3-0

Kuittinen, T. (2012). Apple is getting pushed around by WhatsApp. BGR. Retrieved on August 9, 2013, from http://bgr.com/2012/10/23/apple-imessage-analysis-whatsapp/

Kulka, R. (2011). Web.de-Studie: Marktanteile der Webmail-Dienste – GMX toppt sie alle …. Retrieved on August 9, 2013 from http://www.optivo.de/campfire/web-de-studie-marktanteile-der-webmail-dienste-gmx-toppt-sie-alle/

Kunder, M. de. (2013). The size of the World Wide Web. Retrieved on February 3, 2013 from http://www.worldwidewebsize.com

Lawler, R. (2012). Apple iPad sales topped 100 million two weeks ago. engadget. Retrieved on May 31, 2013 from http://www.engadget.com/2012/10/23/apple-ipad-sales-100-million/

Matzat, L. (2013). Konsequent: Kein Open Data-Portal im Bund. NETZPOLITIK.ORG. Retrieved on August 15, 2013 from https://netzpolitik.org/2013/konsequent-kein-open-data-portal-im-bund/

Max-Planck-Institut für Immaterialgüter- und Wettbewerbsrecht. (2012). Stellungnahme zum Gesetzesentwurf für eine Ergänzung des Urheberrechtsgesetzes durch ein Leistungsschutzrecht für Verleger (p. 8). Retrieved from http://www.ip.mpg.de/files/pdf2/Stellungnahme_zum_Leistungsschutzrecht_fuer_Verleger.pdf

McHugh, J. (2007). Should Web Giants Let Startups Use the Information They Have About You? www.wired.com. Retrieved on December 7, 2012 from http://www.wired.com/techbiz/media/magazine/16-01/ff_scraping?currentPage=all

Medick, V., & Reißmann, O. (2012). Schufa-Plan: Minister wollen Facebook-Schnüffelei stoppen. Spiegel Online. Retrieved on June 24, 2013 from http://www.spiegel.de/netzwelt/netzpolitik/facebook-politiker-wollen-plaene-der-schufa-stoppen-a-837525.html

Molla, R. (2012). Gmail finally beats Hotmail, according to third-party data. GIGAOM. Retrieved on June 27, 2014 from http://gigaom.com/2012/10/31/gmail-finally-beats-hotmail-according-to-third-party-data-chart/

Newark-French, C. (2012). Mobile App Usage Further Dominates Web, Spurred by Facebook. blog.flurry.com. Retrieved on January 13, 2013 from http://blog.flurry.com/bid/80241/Mobile-App-Usage-Further-Dominates-Web-Spurred-by-Facebook

O'Neill, N. (2012). The Forgotten Yahoo Project That Inspired Two Recently Funded Startups. Nick O'Neill Blog. Retrieved on February 16, 2013 from http://nickoneill.com/the-forgotten-yahoo-project-that-inspired-two-recently-funded-startups/

O'Reilly, T. (2007). Pipes and Filters for the Internet. Retrieved on December 7, 2012 from http://radar.oreilly.com/2007/02/pipes-and-filters-for-the-inte.html

Palmer, S. B., & Berners-Lee, T. (2001). Enquire Manual — In HyperText. Retrieved on April 1, 2013 from http://infomesh.net/2001/enquire/manual/#editorial

Peers, M. (2009, December 30). Apple's Hard-to-Swallow Tablet. The Wall Street Journal. Washington, DC. Retrieved from http://online.wsj.com/article/SB10001424052748703510304574626213985068436.html

Petrie, C., & Agarwal, S. (2012). An Alternative to the Top-Down Semantic Web of Services. IEEE Internet Computing, 16(5), 94–97. Retrieved from http://www-cdr.stanford.edu/~petrie/online/peer2peer/semanticscripts.pdf

Plesu, A. (2005). How Big Is the Internet? Softpedia. Retrieved on February 3, 2013 from http://news.softpedia.com/news/How-Big-Is-the-Internet-10177.shtml

Pogue, D. (2010). The Apple iPad: First Impressions. The New York Times. Retrieved on May 31, 2013 from http://pogue.blogs.nytimes.com/2010/01/27/the-apple-ipad-first-impressions/

Reinbold, F. (2012). Lobbyaktion: Google startet Kampagne gegen Leistungsschutzrecht. Spiegel Online. Retrieved on June 6, 2013 from http://www.spiegel.de/netzwelt/netzpolitik/google-startet-kampagne-gegen-leistungsschutzrecht-a-869443.html

Reißmann, O. (2012). Neue Regeln: Twitter verstärkt App-Kontrolle. Spiegel Online. Retrieved on February 17, 2013 from http://www.spiegel.de/netzwelt/web/neue-api-regeln-twitter-verstaerkt-app-kontrolle-a-850564.html

Richter, F. (2013). The Average Smartphone User Has Installed 26 Apps. statista. Retrieved on June 27, 2014 from http://www.statista.com/chart/1435/top-10-countries-by-app-usage/

Robertson, J. (2010). Apple's iPad success is causing PC market pain. Associated Press. Retrieved on May 31, 2013 from http://www.nbcnews.com/id/39660904/ns/technology_and_science-tech_and_gadgets/t/apples-ipad-success-causing-pc-market-pain/

Rubin, J. (2009). Tim Berners-Lee on the Future of His Invention. ON Magazine, (Issue No. 4). Retrieved from http://www.emc.com/leadership/features/berners-lee.htm

Ruiz, E. J., Hristidis, V., Castillo, C., Gionis, A., & Jaimes, A. (2012). Correlating financial time series with micro-blogging activity. Proceedings of the Fifth ACM International Conference on Web Search and Data Mining WSDM 12, 513. doi:10.1145/2124295.2124358

Saylor, M. (2012). The Mobile Wave: How Mobile Intelligence Will Change Everything (p. 304). Vanguard Press.

Shir, E. (2006). Dapper – Unleash your creativity. Dapper Blog. Retrieved on April 11, 2013 from http://dapper.wordpress.com/2006/06/23/dapper-unleash-your-creativity/#comments

Shir, E. (2010). Why Did we sell Dapper to Yahoo? http://shir.posterous.com. Retrieved on December 7, 2012 from http://shir.posterous.com/why-did-we-sell-dapper-to-yahoo

Siegel, D. (2010). Pull — the Power of Semantic Web to Transform your Business. New York, NY: Portofolio, Penguin Publishing Group.

Sippey, M. (2012). Changes coming in Version 1.1 of the Twitter API. Retrieved on June 21, 2013 from https://dev.twitter.com/blog/changes-coming-to-twitter-api

statista. (2014). Number of smartphone users in the U.S. from 2010 to 2018 (in millions). statista. Retrieved from http://www.statista.com/statistics/201182/forecast-of-smartphone-users-in-the-us/

Stiftung Warentest. (2010). Online-Buchung oder Reisebüro. Retrieved on March 29, 2013 from http://www.test.de/Reisen-Die-schoenste-Zeit-des-Jahres-1544406-1546447/

Strickland, J. (n.d.). How Web 3.0 Will Work. howstuffworks. Retrieved on October 25, 2012 from http://computer.howstuffworks.com/web-302.htm

Taylor, M. (2010). iPad Reviews: the Morning-After Edition. The Wall Street Journal. Retrieved on May 31, 2013 from http://blogs.wsj.com/digits/2010/01/28/ipad-reviews-the-morning-after-edition

Teevs, C. (2012). Kreditwürdigkeit: Schufa will Facebook-Nutzer durchleuchten. Spiegel Online.

Thomas, O. (2012). PEAK SEARCH: Why The Google Era May Be Over. www.businessinsider.com. Retrieved on November 11, 2012 from http://www.businessinsider.com/peak-search-google-search-query-decline-2012-10

Tibbets, L. (2010). ifttt the beginning... IFTTT Blog. Retrieved on January 17, 2013 from http://blog.ifttt.com/post/2316021241/ifttt-the-beginning

Website-Monitoring.com. (2012). Facebook 2012 – Facts and Figures. Retrieved on October 7, 2013 from http://www.supermonitoring.com/blog/2012/10/19/facebook-2012-facts-and-figures-infographic/

Wolf, G. (1995). The Curse of Xanadu. Wired Magazine, 3(6), 3.06. Retrieved from http://www.wired.com/wired/archive/3.06/xanadu.html

Wright, R. (1997). THE MAN WHO INVENTED THE WEB. Time Magazin, 149(20), 10–15. Retrieved from http://teaching.cs.uml.edu/~heines/91.513/91.513-2000-01s/resources/tim_berners-lee/time_the_man_who_invented_the_web.htm

Yeung, E. (2010). An Interview with Lisa Gansky – The Art of Business Sharing and Building Strategic Partnership. BizTechDay. Retrieved on February 23, 2013 from http://www.biztechday.com/lisa-gansky-mesh-strategic-partnership-business-of-sharing/

Ziegler, P.-M. (2010). Easyjet unterliegt in Screen-Scraping-Rechtsstreit. heise online. Retrieved from http://www.heise.de/newsticker/meldung/Easyjet-unterliegt-in-Screen-Scraping-Rechtsstreit-1101397.html

Zulla, H. (2012). Habe meine weniger vermögenden Kontakte in Xing, Facebook und G+ entfernt. Die #Schufa kann kommen. Twitter. Retrieved from https://twitter.com/hzulla/status/210622030154969089

www.ingramcontent.com/pod-product-compliance
Lightning Source LLC
Chambersburg PA
CBHW071424050326
40689CB00010B/1967